D0263762

This is the story of the destruction of a talented Jewish family, and of the survival against all the odds of two young sisters. It is one of the most moving stories to emerge from the Second World War. Anita and her elder sister Renate defied death at the hands of the Gestapo and the SS over a period of two and a half years when they were sucked into the whirlpool of Nazi mass extermination, being first imprisoned as 'criminals' and then being transferred, separately, to Auschwitz, and finally to Belsen when the Russians approached. They were saved by their exceptional courage, determination and ingenuity, and by several improbable strokes of luck. At Auschwitz, Anita escaped annihilation through her talents as a cellist when she was co-opted into the camp orchestra directed by Alma Rosé, niece of Gustav Mahler.

Her book is especially remarkable because of the many documents she has managed to preserve, most of them now lodged in the archives of the Imperial War Museum in London. In a sequence of family letters to her sister Marianne, who was marooned in England, from just before the war to 1942 when her parents were deported and liquidated, an atmosphere of happy normality gradually gives way to latent terror and foreboding. The appalling predicament of the Lasker family, and of Anita and Renate in particular when the rest of their relations had been deported and they were left totally alone in Breslau, could not be more poignantly conveyed.

After the liberation of Belsen in April 1945, the correspondence with Marianne in England resumed. Anita was seconded to the British Army, and she quotes first-hand material about the early days of the occupation, including a transcript of part of the Lüneburg trial in late 1945 when she gave evidence about Nazi atrocities at Auschwitz and Belsen, and was confronted in court by her tormentors. In 1946 she and Renate were both finally permitted to emigrate to England. Three years later, Anita became a founder member of the English Chamber Orchestra, in which she still plays the cello.

Inherit the Truth
1939–1945

Anita Lasker-Wallfisch

The Documented Experiences of a Survivor of
Auschwitz and Belsen

Anita Lasker
Wallfisch

dlm

First published in 1996
by Giles de la Mare Publishers Limited
· 3 Queen Square, London WC1N 3AU
Reprinted 1996, 1998

Printed in Great Britain by
Hillman Printers (Frome) Limited
All rights reserved

© Anita Lasker-Wallfisch 1996

Anita Lasker-Wallfisch is hereby identified as author of
this work in accordance with Section 77 of the
Copyright, Designs and Patents Act 1988

A CIP record of this book is available
from the British Library

ISBN 1 900357 01 1

Contents

I dedicate this account of my experiences before, during and after the
Holocaust to my children Raphael and Maya
and my grandchildren Ben, Simon, Joanna and Abraham-Peter

A memorial to my mother and father
and the millions who were silenced and whose stories will never be told;
and a tribute to my sister Renate
and my faithful companions of the camp orchestra
who shared these traumatic years with me

★★★

'And so the survivor told himself that
not to remember was equivalent to becoming the enemy's accomplice:
whosoever contributes to oblivion finishes the killer's work.
Hence the vital necessity to bear witness
lest one find oneself in the enemy's camp.'

From 'A Plea for the Survivors' in Elie Wiesel's *A Jew Today*

Preface

There are many features of this memoir which give pause for thought. From the 'old tattered bundle of letters' which Anita Lasker-Wallfisch re-opened towards what she calls 'the end of my labours', a veritable treasure trove emerged. In it can be seen, on the eve of war, the painful process of failing to obtain the necessary documents, guarantees, etc, to leave Germany. There is a cruel sense of time running out, and of British Jewish bureaucracy fumbling, with lack of funds a constant nagging feature.

Contemporary letters have a tremendous power to recapture the atmosphere of that time, including, even in dark days, the survival of humour. There is also, once war comes in September 1939, the continued survival of hope. Perhaps the enforced move from home will be temporary. Perhaps emigration will still be possible. As late as April 1940 there are hopes that departure from Germany might still be an option, possibly to Italy. On every page the reader, knowing the actual outcome of German Jewry's fate, is gripped by the spell of hindsight.

When Anita's sister Marianne despatches two pounds of coffee from her new home in Britain, it offers all the delights of the 'miracle drink' and the hope of more coffee to come. Hope, like coffee, helped sustain morale. Anita writes: 'Hope was an elixir that kept us going'. But like the coffee, and the travel plans, it was in short supply. In January 1941 a letter from Anita's mother reached her daughter in London. 'Well, perhaps in spite of everything', the mother writes, 'we will all five of us sit down at a cosy round table one day!'

The denouement was long drawn out and cruel. The terrible fate of Germany's Jews was in such violent contrast to their culture and qualities. This book is a testimony to the maintenance of those qualities to the very end. In July 1941 Anita was sixteen years old. There were still elements of normality in Breslau nearly two years after the outbreak of war: her birthday presents included a history of art and an historical atlas, soap and a pair of socks. 'In the afternoon we played quartets.'

In April 1942 Anita's parents were deported. Her grandmother was deported soon afterwards. The destination was unknown; they were never heard of again. With those deportations, all hopes were destroyed. Anita's own path (beginning with a failed attempt, together with her sister Renate, to escape by train to German-occupied Paris) went through Auschwitz to Belsen. In Auschwitz she was in the camp orchestra: to this, she owed her life. 'I may no longer have had a name, but I was identifiable. I could be referred to. I was "the cellist". I had not melted away into the grey mass of nameless, indistinguishable people.'

The moment of liberation for Anita and her sister was at Belsen. 'When the first tank finally rolled into the camp,' Anita writes, 'we looked at our liberators in silence. We were deeply suspicious. We simply could not believe that we had not been blown up before the Allies could get to us.' Like so much in this book, the story of liberation brings a chill to the spine and the realization of the miracle of survival. Anita Lasker-Wallfisch has given an account which, in its personal immediacy, conveys many elements of the almost unconveyable.

Martin Gilbert
Merton College
Oxford
1st March 1996

Acknowledgements

My thanks to Louise Greenberg who asked me for some first-hand information about Theresienstadt for a programme she was preparing for the BBC. I said I could not give her any because I was not there; but if she should want to know about places like Auschwitz and Belsen, I could possibly help. This resulted in the BBC broadcasts about my experiences entitled 'Inherit the Truth', adapted from my original text by Colin McLaren, and an avalanche of letters with inquiries as to where the book could be obtained. They were followed by an unexpected offer to publish what I had originally intended to be for immediate family use only.

I owe special thanks to my publisher and editor Giles de la Mare who with admirable patience made me see that there is a big divide between the spoken and the written word and also that the English language has a lot more grammar than I had given it credit for.

I would also like to thank the Public Record Office who generously permitted me to use the transcript of the Lüneburg trial (ref. WO 235/14, Crown Copyright, reproduced with the permission of the Controller of Her Majesty's Stationery Office); Random House for permission to include the quotation from Elie Wiesel's *A Jew Today*; and everyone who encouraged me to go ahead with this venture.

Illustrations

ILLUSTRATIONS IN TEXT

Key to Names

Alma	Our maid
Auerbach, 'Eierbauch'	Our harmony teacher
Rev Fisher	The Fisher family offered Renate a home in England
Vally and Siegfried Goldschmidt	Relatives living in Switzerland
Grossmama, Grossfloh	My grandmother, Flora Lasker, born in 1861 in New York, and deported in 1942, destination unknown
H & C	Hutchinson & Cuff, a British firm of lawyers
Hadda	Our handicraft teacher
Hanni-Rose Herzberg	A schoolfriend who lived in our house after the deportation of her parents. She worked with us in the paper factory at Sacrau
Jandel, Mariandel	Marianne, my eldest sister (her married name was Adlerstein)
Werner and Ruth Krumme	Friends in whose house we spent our last day in Breslau before trying to escape
Count Künigl	A client of my father's who obtained a special dispensation from the Gestapo to continue representing him in spite of the fact that Jews were no longer permitted to practise law
Edward Lasker, uncle Edward	My father's brother, and a Grand Chessmaster. He was born in 1885 and died in New York in 1983. He had emigrated to America in 1913
Konrad Latte	A friend who supplied me with cyanide, and the brother of my best friend Gabi, who died of diphtheria aged thirteen
Mu, Mutti	My mother
Fräulein Neubert, Püppchen	An employee at the prison in Breslau who supplied us with toy-soldiers to paint
Odette	Our French governess
Re	Renate, my elder sister
Leo Rostal	My cello teacher in Berlin
Helli and Jack Schrier	My cousin and her husband who lived in England
Giuseppe Selmi	First cellist of Radio Rome and prisoner-of-war in a camp near Belsen
Tante Käte and Onkel Ernst Schreiber	My aunt and uncle, into whose flat we moved
Tita, Titel	Anita
Vati, Va	My father
Mrs Wolf and Miss Wanklyn	Ladies in England who tried to help us

Foreword

When I originally wrote the story of my childhood and my 'odyssey', which spanned the years 1933 to 1946 and included the war, prison in Breslau, Auschwitz, Belsen and the destruction of my family, I did it for my children and grandchildren. I had realized as late as 1985 that we had never really talked about those times.

I have often heard that we survivors of the Holocaust 'don't want to talk about it'. I must refute this. The truth is that we are seldom if ever asked about it; and there is also of course the undeniable problem that what we have to tell defies the imagination.

My main aim when I started building a new life for myself after the war, was to catch up on the lost years and provide 'normality' for my children. I believe that most other survivors felt the same way. It took me many years to understand that normality is not something you can create out of nothing. How can there be normality when you hesitate to answer your children's questions about where their grandma and grandpa are for fear of traumatizing them beyond redemption – because the answer would be that they are lying in a mass grave somewhere in Poland? Providing normality for my children meant that among other things they should not feel different or isolated.

Now, fifty years later, I know that this was all a pipedream. There is no place in normal life for stories which are so outrageously horrendous that they seem like fairy tales at best, and gross exaggerations at worst.

I had many illusions when I was liberated. I thought that our suffering was an atonement for all time, and that the generations to come would be free from prejudice for ever. Alas, I was wrong. There are many people today, not all of them stupid or uneducated, who maintain that the Holocaust is a serious distortion of the facts, or even a complete lie.

Some forty years after the events took place I began scribbling down notes about them whenever I had the time to spare. I did much of it in airports or on aeroplanes, making use of dead time; and I eventually compiled a 'book' for my children so that they could 'inherit the truth' and keep alive the memory of those terrible days. That 'book' has formed the basis for this published volume.

The book contained many photographs and letters that came into my possession seven years after the war ended. They had belonged to my eldest sister Marianne, the only member of my family to escape from Germany. Maybe it was providence, but near the end of my labours, I had occasion to open my 'grey box' (you will hear more about it later), and there I found, not what I was looking for, but an old tattered bundle of letters tied up with string. I had forgotten they were in my possession. They were in fact all the letters our family had written to Marianne, who had gone to England shortly before the outbreak of war. They are from my mother and father, my sister Renate and myself, and date back to 1939, 1940, 1941 and 1942. There they stop. Renate's and my letters start again in 1945. With some difficulty I have translated them all. A major quandary has been that in translation a great deal tends to get lost, especially the humour – yes, believe it or not, there was quite a lot of humour there.

Ironically and very sadly, Marianne died in childbirth in 1952, and the letters and photographs were passed on to me by her husband.

I shall use excerpts from these letters to substantiate my account. After war broke out, our letters were sent to Marianne via Switzerland and America, and occasionally via Holland. Some of them were undated; and we used a sort of cover language in them to disguise their real origin. We also had to filter out many things that were too dangerous to talk about.

Introduction

I have never, as it happens, had an overwhelming desire to talk about my experiences. The reasons for this are complex and varied, but I have certainly not had any desire to forget. However, there seems to be a taboo on the subject of the Holocaust.

When we first came to England, Renate and I badly wanted to talk, but *no one* asked us any questions. I know very well that, on the whole, people want to protect themselves from too much knowledge. Under the pretext of not wanting to bring back memories – in case they should be upsetting – they allow silence to prevail. There is actually no way that such memories *can* be brought back. Apart from certain details, there is nothing to bring back, since your experiences have never left you in the first place. When you have seen and gone through what we have, those experiences become an integral part of you, and they inevitably colour your whole make-up.

We were aware that we were a bit of a disappointment in some ways. We had ceased to look like ex-Belsen internees and we definitely did not need any medical attention. It had taken us eleven months to get permission to come to England. (We were liberated on 15th April 1945; we finally left Belsen on 27th December; we got stuck in Brussels; and we ultimately reached England on 18th March 1946.) It is not surprising that we looked like reasonably normal people by then. Very probably it would have been easier to ply us with food than listen to our stories. I don't mean to criticize, but I would just like to tell it as it was. Soon the magic moment passed. We no longer felt like talking and settled for a kind of isolation which in time became second nature.

There have of course been occasions when people have had the courage to ask questions. I have always answered them willingly, usually by relating some amusing episode or telling them about one of those strange coincidences with which my life seems to have been so richly endowed.

Much has been written about concentration camps and the atrocities committed by the Germans. There is little that I can add. I don't know how to describe *hunger*, not the type everybody is familiar with when a meal has been skipped but hunger that causes actual *pain*; or what it is like to be *cold* without any prospect of ever becoming warm again; or the sensation of *real fear* and total misery.

One of the reasons for my reticence is the acute humiliation I feel when, trying to put into words some of the unspeakable things that have happened, I encounter boredom or disbelief. I feel humiliated on behalf of the millions of the dead, and I also feel guilty. It is the age-old guilt of survivors who wonder why they should be in a position to talk at all.

So if you have been a witness to this twentieth-century outrage of sophisticated cruelty of man to man, you will inevitably live in some kind of limbo, cut off from the rest of the world. I have accepted the reality that there are those who 'know' and those who 'don't know'; and there the story seems to end.

It was something that happened in Rome a few years ago when I was there on a concert tour, that prompted me to make my first attempt at recording some of the absurd coincidences and adventures that have coloured my life. On returning to my hotel late one night, I met two young colleagues at the bar, and they asked me how I had spent the evening. I told them I had spent it with somebody I had not seen since the liberation of Belsen, and related the circumstances under which I had originally met him. I was amazed at the impact the story made on my young friends, and at their genuine interest. I had to *promise* them to try to put something down on paper. It led me to wonder whether I might be able to make some contribution, however insignificant, to help commemorate an era.

My book will not be an account of the horrors themselves, nor mainly an historical document. The subject of the Holocaust has been treated many times with varying degrees of success. I merely want to put on paper how *my* life has been affected by having lived in Germany at the time of the Third Reich, as a Jew.

Pre-war Germany and the Kristallnacht

My earliest recollection of there being something amiss must have been around 1933. Up to then I had had a sheltered and extremely happy life. I was my parents' third daughter much to the dismay of my father, who wanted three sons. My father was a lawyer of some repute, and my mother, apart from being very beautiful, had many accomplishments. She was exceptionally clever with her hands and made all our clothes herself. But most important, she was a fine violinist. I remember vividly the cosy feeling I had lying in bed listening to her practising. She usually started her practising routine with the opening octaves of the Beethoven Concerto. My father loved singing and we had a lot of chamber music in the house. All three of us learned instruments. My eldest sister Marianne played the piano and Renate the violin. I was the cellist. We were a trio and as a special treat I was occasionally allowed to take part in the weekly quartet sessions at home. We were encouraged to speak French and had a French governess for a while. My father had a great love of languages. He maintained that people have as many souls as they have languages. He was very anxious that we should not forget the French we had learned while the governess was with us, and it was a rule in our house that on Sundays only French was spoken. In my youthful ignorance I considered this to be absolutely ridiculous, and so never opened my mouth on Sundays.

Life was pretty good, and it seemed inconceivable that it should not go on like that for ever. I suppose ours was a typical middle-class assimilated Jewish family. There was little emphasis on our Jewishness, but I remember that my parents went to synagogue on the high holidays and that we spent Pessach, the festival commemorating the deliverance of the Jews from Egypt, at my maternal grandmother's home.

Although life proceeded fairly normally, we had a growing awareness that all was not well. There were worried faces and there was talk of emigration. I was too young to understand what it was all about, but I knew that something bad had happened. I had my first encounter with anti-semitism. A fellow pupil in the small private school I attended would snatch the sponge from me as I was about to wipe the blackboard, and say: 'don't let the Jew have the sponge'; or children would spit at me in the street and call me a 'dirty Jew'. Since we had been scarcely conscious of our Jewishness at home, I found this all very bewildering and was full of envy for people who did not have this mysterious stigma.

The years went by, and the segregation of Jews and Aryans increased steadily.

I remember certain laws coming into force. All Jewish females had to add the name 'Sarah', and all males the name 'Israel', to their signature. We were no longer allowed to employ household help under the age of forty-five for fear of Rassenschande, racial pollution. Jews had to attend Jewish schools, and the infamous notice 'JUDEN UNERWÜNSCHT', 'Jews not welcome', appeared more and more frequently in public places like restaurants and cinemas. Our lives were being very gradually undermined – so gradually that, alas, the real threat behind it all could be ignored by over-optimistic people. My father was one of them. He was convinced that this nonsense would end one day soon, 'when the Germans come to their senses'. However, many of our friends did leave the country, and even my own family began talking of emigration.

But where could we go? How could we obtain the necessary papers? My father's profession was a serious obstacle. He was trained in a legal system which was confined to Germany. How could he possibly earn a living in another country?

The first colossal indication of impending disaster was on 9th November 1938 when Herr vom Rath, a minor official at the German Embassy in Paris, was killed by a Jew by the name of Grynspan. This incident 'spontaneously enraged the German people', as the press put it at the time, and the first major pogrom of the Nazi era took place. Synagogues were burnt down and Jewish shops were smashed up and looted. They were easy to recognize. The owners had to display the Star of David and their name in regulation-size letters on their shop windows. There was no mistaking a Jewish shop for an Aryan one.

The majority of the male population was arrested and the expression 'concentration camp' became part of the vocabulary. More and more people left the country, an undertaking which became increasingly difficult, or just disappeared.

Every day that came to an end with one's family still intact was a kind of achievement. My father escaped arrest on that notorious Kristallnacht (night of the shattered glass), as it became known, on 9th November thanks to the courage of a great friend of ours, Walter Mathias Mehne, a violin-maker in Breslau. He was not a Jew, and he deliberately ignored the fact that the streets were crawling with members of the Gestapo looking for Jews. He climbed the stairs to our flat, took my father with him, and drove him around the town in his car for the rest of the day. He could easily have been stopped and found himself in an embarrassing and highly dangerous position. The courage of a man like Mehne is all the more noteworthy since he was a well-known figure in Breslau. His premises – it was a 'father and son' business – were situated on the first floor of a building on the Tauentzien Platz, right in the centre of the town. It was at once recognizable from its red violin-shaped signs which hung in the windows. It was much more a meeting point for musicians than a mere shop, and a great many of those musicians were committed Nazis. Notwithstanding this, the Mehnes were steadfast in their refusal to hang up a picture of Hitler inside, although that was expected of every good citizen.

They also refused to hang out a swastika on the various 'flag days'. It all made them instantly suspect. But they would not yield an inch. They disapproved of what was happening and were not afraid to show it. Both father and son conducted themselves in a manner which can only be called exemplary. There were indeed some Germans – sadly not enough of them – whose behaviour was beyond reproach.

At that particular moment I was not at home but in Berlin, where I had been sent to study the cello with Leo Rostal. In retrospect, I much admire my parents' decision to send a mere child off on her own to a big city like Berlin. It was in reality the only way I could have had cello lessons.

In Breslau, which was a much smaller place, we could not find a teacher brave enough to teach a Jewish child. It might have been observed and had dire consequences. So it had been arranged that I should go to Berlin; and since I was far too young to leave school, permission had to be obtained for me to have private tuition in school subjects so that I could devote my time to practising. I was barely thirteen years old. Things did not quite work out the way my parents had probably envisaged. I had a room in the apartment of an old lady who was supposed to tutor me in school subjects for two hours every morning and generally keep an eye on me. Everything in it was terribly old-fashioned – and rather frightening at first. My room contained fifty-seven pictures; and I had meatballs and brussels sprouts nearly every day.

I soon got used to it and had a great time. I did the minimum amount of practising and loved wandering about in the large department store, the KDW. I felt extremely grown up.

I enjoyed my cello lessons very much and had a good friend in my teacher. I learned a lot from him, smoking included. It all stood me in good stead for the vacuum of the next eight years: my stay in Berlin was doomed to come to an end after only six months. As I have said, I was there on 9th November, and I recall very anxious telephone conversations with my mother that evening. I was not able to remain in Berlin. Leo Rostal emigrated to the States, and I went home. It was no time for a family to be separated voluntarily.

My eldest sister Marianne managed to leave Germany in the nick of time. She was an ardent Zionist and had always wanted to go to Palestine. She had done an apprenticeship as a carpenter, a most unusual thing for a girl at that time. She had had many bitter fights with my parents about it. They had not yet come to terms with the fact that the days when one's aim was to go to university were over. Marianne was determined that her role in life was to emigrate to Palestine and help build up that country in a practical way. For some reason she went to England as the first stage of her journey to Palestine. I believe this had something to do with a chil-drens' transport which she was meant to accompany. She did not reach her ultimate destination until much later ... Shortly after her arrival in England, war was declared, on 3rd September. She spent the war years in England making herself useful. She became a member of a working party, otherwise all male, which went round the country doing repair work. Her speciality was roof-thatching and she was much in demand.

2

The Destruction of a Family

Attempts to arrange emigration before the outbreak of war
Life after 9th November continued more or less normally, although one's concept of normality was somewhat distorted by then.

The letters written to Marianne convey the general atmosphere of those days better than I can describe them now. I wrote this letter to her in June 1939:

Breslau, 3rd June 1939

... This morning at 7 o'clock I took Eva to the station. Our meetings [of the Jewish Youth Organization] now consist of Steffi, Susi, Eva and myself. We did not sing at all. We read *Cornet* (Rilke) and talked about war ...

Now only Steffi is left ... For the Herzl-Bialik celebration at the school, I played *Nigun* and two movements of the Marcello Sonata ... It was very nice. All the teachers say 'Sie' to me! I invited Hoffmann [a teacher] to our Thursday quartet evening. As 'thanks' he made me a present of some super music ...

Konrad has written to you twice. He *urgently* needs a certificate to say that he is a member of the 'Werkleute' [the name of our youth movement]. Why don't you answer? His case is getting more and more pressing. Things look blacker and blacker here. Please take this seriously. So much can result from negligence. Maybe a letter got lost ...

The other day I went to Hoppe to buy some music. As I was browsing through this and that, I came across some music by Bruch. The little man behind the counter whispered very softly into my ear: 'Take this before I tear it up.' As I look a little closer, what do I see? *Kol Nidrei* by Bruch! It should have cost 2.50 marks, and he gave it to me as a present! What do you say to that? You ask me what I do all day: I practise, and twice a week I have English lessons. Also I am trying to continue with French. ... On Tuesdays and Thursdays I go to the sports-ground. Now they have days for boys and days for girls. The boys have three days naturally and the girls two. Utterly disgusting! ... That's all for today ... Write by return!

Yours ... A

My mother wrote these letters:

Breslau, 19th June 1939

... The general mood of the family is not exactly rosy. The letter from England has depressed us very much. I hope that everything will sort itself out. If it doesn't, then I don't know what we are going to do ... We have not had any news from Edward for a long time. Not a very encouraging sign. If only there were some prospects for the children! They should both get into a routine soon ... Since I always hope for something out of the ordinary, perhaps the letter to C will have a measure of success after all ... In any case, Mariandel, do everything in your power to help us ... Couldn't you ask E once more about the families she found earlier for the children? ... Do whatever you can for your sisters and for us. You have got the photographs – show them around! ... One really has to try *everything!*

So my dear child, keep well. With lots of kisses,

Your Mu

Breslau, 26th July 1939

Dear Marianne,

Yesterday's letter from you brought much interesting news ... I hardly dare hope for us – although I have not lost all confidence in a favourable outcome yet. If only there was a little hope for Anita and Renate ... I would be so happy. It would be wonderful if Anita could get to her longed-for tuition with Casals ... You know what would be most important for Renate ... It would be wrong to put her in too much of a strait-jacket. She has the nature of a little bird which could be harmed if its wings were too severely clipped ... Keep well! Mariandel. Many greetings ...

Yours, Mutti

More and more restrictions crept in for Jews, and slowly even incurable optimists like my father began to realize that time was running out. Increasingly frantic attempts at emigration were being made but, as usual in such situations, fewer and fewer countries were prepared to accept immigrants. The conditions that had to be met became almost impossible to fulfill. The letters my father and mother wrote to Marianne in London during that period will give you a more comprehensive picture of our desperate last-minute attempts to get out of Germany, and of the hopes that were raised – only to be dashed, as time went by. The United States had a quota system that allowed a certain number of people to enter it from other countries. My father was born in Kempen (Posen) which automatically put him on the Polish quota. Our number was so low on the list that our turn would probably have come up twenty-five years too late.

We had various connections in England, some professional ones, which explain the letters to Hutchinson and Cuff, and some personal ones too. Here, first of all, are a few of the more formal letters my father wrote in his touchingly bad English, obviously with the help of a dictionary, and a selection of the replies. They convey the hopeless struggle in which he was engaged.

[written in English]

Dr Lasker, Breslau 13, Kaiser Wilhelm Str 69 *20th July 1939*

COPY

German Jewish Aid Committee
Woburn House-Upper Woburn Place,
London WC1

I thank you for your letter of the 17th July.

In view of the good chances which you attributed to my application in your letter of the 22nd of June, my hopes have been very disillusioned by your last decision.

In the meantime my brother [Edward] wrote me from New York on the 2nd of July as follows: ' ... The Committee would have no success with the British Government, *unless a sufficient deposit would be made in London* to cover the expenses for your living during the next five years at least ... and that will be a little over $5000 altogether.

... I can only suppose that no acknowledgement of the deposit which my cousin in Basel payed [*sic*] to you at the Midland Bank on the 9th of May, has come to your deeds ...

Further I have noted that you only stated in your letter of 17th inst. my high waiting number for America without expressing your opinion about my eventual plans for re-emigration to Palestine ...

With regard to all those circumstances I ask you to let me kindly know if you are willing to make a further examination of my case ...

I am yours faithfully,

Signed Dr Lasker

[written in English]

Strasse der SA 69   *Breslau, 23rd July 1939*

Dear Mrs. Wolf,

I beg to inform you that we have got a refuse [*sic*] from the Aid Committee in London, owing to our high waiting number for America. The committee asks me to present alternative plans for re-emigration ...

We are very discouraged by this answer and are now forced to get out our children as quick as possible.

Fortunately we have got a good chance to settle our youngest daughter Anita in France, where she would be able to continue her studies on the violoncello. We hope this chance will be realized, so that only Renate – fifteen and a half years old – would have to be settled in England. Perhaps it would be easier to find hospitality for my daughter Renate, if I inform you that she would get a security of £50 and that it would be no more necessary to make a deposit for her ...

I am so sorry to trouble you with my great sorrows again; but the new turn of things made the situation for my children more urgent than ever. We are very thankful to you that you took matters in hand ...

I am yours very sincerely,

Signed Alfons Lasker

[written in English]

Dr Lasker, Breslau 13, Kaiser Wilhelm Strasse 69 *Breslau, 5th August 1939*

Ms Hutchinson & Cuff
Solicitors
London WC2

Dear Sirs,

I thank you for your letter from July 24th. Just now I received from the committee the following advice, which is discouraging me again:

' ... We thank you for your letter of 20th of July and if you would be good enough to send us your full plans for emigration to Palestine and a copy of your landing permit, we shall be pleased to continue with your application ... '

... Actually I am not able to present a landing certificate for Palestine; moreover the immigration there has been barred till the 1st of April 1940 ...

Perhaps it would be suitable as well to direct the attention of the committee on the actual negotiations in Washington endeavouring to facilitate the emigration to USA. As my brother is *an American citizen* we may account that it will be our turn in a short time for getting a preference quota ...

Fortunately my flat has not been hired yet so far, and I am trying to prolong the agreement with my landlord for three months.

I am looking forward to your further news with tension,

Yours faithfully,

Signed Dr Lasker

[written in English]

COPY   *Breslau, 15th August 1939*

Dear Miss Wanklyn,

... We know by Mrs Wolf that we have to thank that invitation to your deep interest in our situation and to your endless troubles. It is so difficult for us to express our thankfulness in the English language as we should like to do. But let me add that we thank you especially so much for taking up a moral guarantee for Renate at Mr and Mrs Fisher, and for her further care after her being over there. You may be sure that Renate will not disappoint yourself and Mrs Wolf ... All that we heard and saw showed us a very sympathetic family. We are happy that Renate will go to them. We have no scruples in the point of religion and are fully trusting in the tact of the family Fisher.

It stands to reason that the £50 which our relations can give for Renate will be available on behalf of Rev Fisher if it is not necessary to make a deposit with the Aid Committee. It was so kind of you and Mrs Wolf that you proposed to bring up the sum yourself eventually; but it would be very painful to us to be charging you with costs, after all the troubles which we have caused you in this matter and you are willing to take up in future on behalf of Renate ... I wrote a detailed letter to Mr and Mrs

Fisher; I could not finish it before Sunday, as I am not able to write an English letter without the aid of a dictionary ...

As I wrote to Mr Fisher it will be probably possible for Renate to arrive over there about the middle of September.

I am writing to you a typed letter, because you will have difficulties enough to understand my beginner English. I shouldn't like to double these difficulties by my handwriting. Let me repeat once more our deep and heartfelt thanks. We hope to be able to express our gratitude personally one day.

Yours very sincerely,

Signed A Lasker

And here are some replies that my father received:

Dr A Lasker
Kaiser Wilhelm Str 69
Breslau 13
Germany   *17th July 1939*

Dear Sir,

Further to your letter of the 22nd of June, and yours of the 11th July, enquiring as to the position of your case, we regret to inform you that we are unable to proceed with the matter in view of your very high waiting number for America.

In view of this decision we advise you to endeavour to obtain alternative plans for re-emigration and on receipt of such information, we assure you that we will do our utmost to assist you.

Yours faithfully

German Jewish Aid Committee ...

18th July 1939

Dear Dr Lasker,

A letter from Miss Lindsay reached me some weeks ago. This letter asks my help to get your two daughters aged fifteen and thirteen over to England. It was impossible for me to extend an invitation to them to come to me, but I have been and still am doing all I can to help your daughters.

At present I can report nothing definite. Please don't take my long silence for indifference. I am continuing to do all in my power to help and will write to you immediately if I am successful.

Signed R Wolf

Nothing seemed to succeed. At the last moment my father had tried in desperation to get at least Renate and myself out.

A family had been found who were willing to take Renate. It was that of a certain Rev Mr Fisher, and preparations appeared to have gone far enough for the colour of a school uniform for Renate to be discussed. This is what my father wrote to Rev Fisher (in English):

Breslau, 12th August 1939

Dear friends,

The contents of your letter and the manner how you offer to us the hospitality in your home for Renate encourages me to return your kind address. I read out your letter twice to my family and each time I saw some tears in the eyes of my wife.

The same day I received a letter from Mrs Wolf, the next day a report from Marianne, and two days after a letter from Miss W. We are quite embarrassed still by so much goodness and it is not easy for me to find the right words – especially in a foreign language – expressing our real feelings.

You tell us in your letter that many Jews on the continent have seen a poor representation of what Christianity really is. On reading these words I remembered involuntarily the situation of distress in which Schiller once received a letter from the Duke of Augustenburg with the quite unexpected offer of an annual pension. I would reply to you the same as Schiller did to the Duke: 'One sole noble deed restores the belief in pure humanity that is beaten down by so many examples of reality.'

... We are very glad to send you our daughter, fully trusting to the spirit of your home that we have met in your letter. In these days I also read your two writings you have been kind enough to enclose, and I believe to find there, in metaphors, the same ideas which your letter expresses in the language of heart. We have no scruples regarding your opinions about what Renate will be able to do, without any distinction between herself and Nancy. We think that the customs of faith are less important than its spirit. Should it have merely been fortuitousness that you quoted, at the end of your letter, a sentence of Christ which Hillel has marked – with nearly the same words, I think – as the chief truth of the Jewish faith?

At last I take the liberty to speak with you about some practical points: I hope to get the permit for Renate to enter your country till the end of August. But the formalities to be fulfilled here might take about three or four weeks. So Renate will hardly be able to leave Germany before the

10th of September. [War broke out on 1st September in Germany, and 3rd September in England.]

As far as we are informed, a certain school dress is prescribed in England. As it is rather impossible to transfer any money from Germany into a foreign country, it would be very good to make the dress here. My wife could do it herself, if you kindly would send us a sketch and a pattern. We should be thankful too for some instructions about stockings, shoes, hat, and the like.

Further, it would be a special pleasure for us to know some wishes of Nancie [*sic*]. The only use of money possible to us is to buy some things which are allowed to take along. So we should like to give a pleasure to your daughter Nancie.

We hope that Nancie and Renate shall become good friends. Renate is a jolly and sociable girl. She feels well what kind of home she is going to enter, and will do all to prove herself thankful to you.

We well understand all that you had written to us in English and German; but in writing myself an English letter I feel rather insecure ...

We have been very pleased, after receiving your letter, to make your personal acquaintance 'in effigie'. We shall beg to send you our own photos on occasion.

With hearty thanks for all your kindness and with friendly greetings to yourself and Nancie,

Yours very sincerely,

Alfons Lasker

I myself had had some prospect of going to Paris. At that point we could not have known that this would not have helped me very much anyway. But it was now too late for us all, and we were well and truly stuck in Germany. We were an extremely close family, and I do not recall any particular friction. I can honestly say that I had a very happy childhood and if there were clouds, they were the result of these outside circumstances.

I remember our home as being well organized. We lived in a spacious flat and we seemed to give each other plenty of space in every sense of the word. There was a general absence of rules at home, and yet there were some rules which were not to be broken: no child was ever allowed to sit on an armchair for example; you did not 'slouch'; nor did you sit around 'doing nothing' ... I can hear my parents' voices now saying: *'do something'*. There was no question of our sitting around and doing nothing. I have not really got over this even now, and I feel distinctly guilty if I ever have the desire to read a book in the middle of the day. Considering that we must have been comfortably off – we had two maids at one time – we lived very frugally.

One unassailable institution in our family was the Saturday afternoon 'Kaffee und Kuchen' (coffee and cake). We would all gather without fail round the table, drink coffee and have a wonderful choice of Zehnpfennigstücke (small individual pieces of patisserie); and my father would read to us or tell us stories about the war and the trenches. I am referring to the First World War of course. I made my first acquaintance with Goethe's *Faust* that way, and we continued this tradition until the bitter end.

To leap forward for a moment, in this letter written to Marianne in July 1940 my father refers to those Saturday afternoons mentioning that we had just finished reading *Don Carlos*. In order to appreciate the qualities of a man like my father, you must remember that the backdrop to these cultural pursuits was war and the threat of deportation.

He wrote (I have translated this):

… You will have heard by now that our beautiful travel plans have yet again come to nothing at the very last minute. We were all completely ready to go. Maybe this is just a postponement. Maybe … You may be interested to hear that we have reinstated our old tradition of Saturday afternoon 'coffee and cake' in the past two months – although in a somewhat altered format. The coffee is followed by a drama reading. (Sometimes we do it in the evening.) At first we read *Don Carlos* and then we dared approach *Faust*. We have just finished the first part. I think it was a good idea. All the participants got a lot of enjoyment from it …

I knew that I was the object of a lot of envy from my friends for the great personal freedom I had within my family. I always had a key to the house, even when I was very young, and I never had to give a detailed account of my movements. Not a common thing in those days. There was much mutual trust and an absence of pressure within the family. It is only now, in retrospect, that it seems remarkable to me that my parents sent me to Berlin on my own when I was so young. I doubt whether I made the best of my study time there, but I had no way of knowing how short-lived that opportunity was going to be. Once back in Breslau, I felt very much at a loss. Some more abortive attempts were made to find me a cello teacher: even a return to Berlin was contemplated and more or less arranged. By that time Jews needed permission from the Gestapo to travel. I can recall going to the Gestapo HQ to ask for this permission. I was promptly thrown out.

On 26th August 1939 my father wrote to Marianne (translated):

... I returned from Berlin yesterday. Now, with one blow everything has changed. My detailed letter has long become obsolete on account of events. A letter followed me to Berlin with a personal guarantee for Anita from Odette's brother. Too late! In Breslau I found your letter with the idea for Chile ... too late! This morning the Unbedenklichkeits-bescheinigung [a document stating that you have fulfilled the requirements for emigration] for Renate and Anita arrived ... Everything was too late! I am sharing Mutti's hope that you will manage to get on by yourself. Renate's protectors, who can no longer protect her, will no doubt be a support for you ... You need not worry about us. If the post should be cut off one of these days, we will probably be able to send letters via neutral countries. In any case, you can send letters via uncle S in Basel, Pelicanweg 5, and ask him to forward them. We will do the same. Renate and Anita are our big worries. For them to have to let everything go now when they are so near to reaching their goal, is bitter. I still have not given up hope for England. Perhaps permits and visas can be obtained through neutral countries.

But in the end everything personal is irrelevant vis à vis the question of what is going to happen to Europe, and to Palestine! My usual optimism has become somewhat shaky. At the moment the situation is so untransparent that one has to muster enormous patience, and wait ...

Dear Marianne ... keep well. Many, many kisses ...

Your father

My mother wrote this to Marianne:

... It is unlikely we will hear from each other for a long time now, and we will miss your news very much. We are especially sad for Renate. It would all have been too perfect really. Yesterday we even had two wonderful letters from the Fishers! ... You have so many good friends over there that you will not be abandoned ... I am missing work dreadfully. It is a necessity of life for me ... For today I just want to say my wish for you and for us too is that we will see each other again soon.

Yours M

And I wrote:

My dearest sister, I hope that I may still have a reply from you to my letters. But everything is so meaningless now. I hope it all can still be prevented.

With a thousand good wishes and thoughts, I am with you,

Yours Anita

And Renate wrote this:

… Now, after all, nothing is going to come of our reunion! We are all a little mixed up, which is hardly surprising. We are still hoping …

Family life after having to leave our home

War broke out in Germany on 1st September 1939, as I have said. I remember the day very well. I looked out of the window and was surprised I could not see any fighting or hear any shooting. In fact everything looked just as it had before. My father *still* had not given up hope. There was still some scheme afoot to go to Italy, and we were buoyed up by these false hopes for a considerable time. In fact right up to April or May 1940.

My mother wrote this letter to Marianne on 6th November 1939, via Holland:

My dearest Mariandel,

It was such a joy for us seeing your handwriting again after so long. It has improved slightly, by the way. We are so happy that you are well and that you are in your element in your work … Soon there will be great disorder here. We have to vacate the flat on the 15th and pack most of our things beforehand.

We are moving to Tante Käte [my mother's sister], who has offered us three rooms and the maid's room. I hope that this will work all right and that it will not be for any length of time. We will take some of the furniture so that we can make it a little bit cosy. The children want to tell you lots of things, so I am closing this letter with many kisses.

… Yours Mu

So we had to vacate our lovely home and move in with my mother's sister and her husband, who was a most disagreeable man. But the move, which was a drastic change in our circumstances, was underpinned by the optimistic thought that it was only a temporary measure.

My father wrote as follows on 25th March 1940 (Breslau was no longer mentioned):

... In the past two weeks I have worked like a madman ... Unfortunately one overestimates the speed of the procedures somewhat and the earliest day for our trip should be 15th April ...

If you could still send two pounds of coffee to us *here*, that would be wonderful ...

Marianne had obviously been able to send us some parcels. The coffee in particular must have seemed like an apparition from another world.

My mother to Marianne on 6th April 1940:

My dearest M,

It really was such a joy when your parcel arrived here today. There are such unimaginable delicacies in it and we are savouring everything with special enjoyment. It arrived just at the right time because Vati has been completely run down these last few weeks, and now I can feed him up a bit. The 'miracle drink' always stimulates him, and Anita has fits when she smells the lovely aroma. Many, many thanks from all of us ... We still have not fixed the day of our departure. It merely depends on a few formalities and, apart from that, Vati is so exhausted that he has to go to bed for a few hours during the day and can only work in a limited way. Since yesterday he has perked up a little, and we hope very much to be able to travel on the 18th or 20th. Anita and I keep having to have farewell music evenings. When we have gone, quartet playing will be out of the question. There are no violinists or cellists here any more, and when we'll be able to get a quartet together again is more than uncertain ... Our present circumstances are most unpleasant ...

In her next letter, sent on the occasion of Marianne's birthday, she wrote:

... Now, after all, this birthday letter is still being written to you from here. Things don't always work out the way you think! But on your actual birthday [28th April], I hope that you will be able to send your thoughts to us in Bolzano, and that we will drink a bottle of Chianti to your health ...

However, in July that year my father wrote to Marianne – in the letter already quoted – saying that at the very last minute our travel plans had come to nothing once more.

All I remember today about that crisis is that we were sitting in an office, probably the Italian Embassy, all eager and full of nervous tension as the official kept turning our documents over and over, the rubber stamp in his hand, and almost ready to validate our passports, and then decided not to bring the stamp down on its intended target for reasons which I no longer recall, and which are of no importance now anyway. The only thing that mattered was that our hopes, raised so high, were dashed yet again. I have no idea what precisely my father was expecting from life in Italy, which was after all allied to Germany. But since we never got there, it is barely worthwhile speculating. I can still sense the appalling tension in that embassy and our terrible disappointment as we went home, visa-less.

I gather now, as I re-read the letters, that even then my father had not given up hope. Hope was an elixir that kept us going. So we went on trying, war or no war. Apart from the ever-increasing persecution and restrictions on our lives as Jews, which we had got used to, we could almost pretend that there was a status quo which might last indefinitely.

We tried to reconcile ourselves to having to remain in Germany, and we took up all sorts of activities. I had lessons in harmony and played a lot of chamber music. We did not like our new home much, but we were not as desperate as we should have been. Life at my aunt's and uncle's flat proved pretty disastrous eventually. However, we were extremely lucky that we had anywhere to go at all after having to leave our home.

My mother wrote to Marianne on 15th January 1941:

… The four of us are still together here. Tita [my nickname] has not run away any more [this relates to my abortive attempt to go back to Berlin to continue my studies]. The co-habitation with K and E and dog is not always pure joy. But it would be difficult for us to find a small flat and also we would have scarcely anything left to furnish it with. Alma [our maid] is no longer with us and we manage the household between us. Because of this I rarely get to my violin, but I do try to keep in practice somehow by playing chamber music. Fortunately I still have a sewing machine and I have even been making things for people outside the immediate family … I often sit with the children in their minute room. They sing canons for me and try very hard to teach me the third part. Or else Renate tells us about a film or some other nonsense, and we always say: ' … if only Jandel was here now!' Anita then imitates you: do you remember how you used to fall into her bed, cheeks blown out and crumpled up with sleep, and how you used to talk nonsense for hours on end?

We never knew how marvellous everything was then!!!

Well, perhaps, in spite of everything, we will all five of us sit down at a cosy round table again one day!

I go back to school

Finally, then, it became painfully obvious that we were not going anywhere. It was now 1941. I had got fed up with hanging around, doing this and that without much purpose, and I decided to go back to school. I had lost nearly two years and had to make a major effort to catch up with my lessons.

I wrote this letter to Marianne on the same day as my mother wrote to her:

15th January 1941

My sweet dear little Marianne,

I cannot express in words how madly happy we were to have your letter. Everybody ran together when we heard Mutti's cry. Vati immediately took the letter and left us in such suspense – because of your catastrophic handwriting, it reached an unbelievable pitch.

Since I only have very little space left, I will not waste it on preliminaries.

I suppose you think that I am pursuing my cello studies – far from it! For two weeks I have been back at school. When you come round from your unavoidable fainting fit, you may read on: I made this decision when I couldn't stand being idle any longer, and a continuation of my cello studies unfortunately proved impossible. Crazy as I am, I have of course exaggerated everything madly, and made up two years of school in four weeks, so that I am now in the same age group as when I left. Namely: Obersekunda. But I have to take an entrance exam, and the day before yesterday I did Latin and German. Next week it goes on. I am already the best in class in Latin. Of the people you know, only fat Susi is left. The school is very cosy now. We all sit around tables and, because of lack of space, we go to school in the afternoon. We have no longer had our old school building for about four weeks. You would hardly know any of the teachers. Only three of the old guard are still there. You will no doubt be flabbergasted by all these happenings! But so as to avoid being entirely unfaithful to the muses of music, I have heroically resumed my studies with our friend Eierbauch. [His real name was Auerbach. 'Eierbauch' means 'Eggtummy'.] Either he has changed, or I have forfeited part of my stupidity. In any case, we are getting on famously now, and I have already learned a lot with him.

What it cost me in terms of courage to go back to him, you can just imagine! If you can remember those days, I suffered from a real 'Eierbauch delusion' ... The Lattes are moving in the next few days [they went into hiding in Berlin] ... You have not forgotten that the second anniversary of Gabi's death was on 5th January and she would have been sixteen on the 28th? [Gabi Latte was Konrad Latte's sister and she had been my best friend. We were inseparable. She died of diphtheria and scarlet fever on 5th January 1938. These were pre-penicillin days.]

Excuse my terrible handwriting and this confused letter. I am awfully tired. I have worked rather a lot these last weeks. I try so often to picture what it would be like if you suddenly came into the room, and I think it is high time this moment materialized ... I would kiss you innumerable times on your sweet round cheeks just as I always used to do after lunch when you woke up and came into the room with your hair all rumpled up. I greet and kiss you with all my heart.

Yours Anita

And my father sent this letter:

24th January 1941

Dearest Mariandel,

Your December letter came a week after the November one ...

It was such a pleasure to have news from you after so unexpectedly short an interval ... The children have already told you quite a lot. The biggest piece of news is that Anita is going to school again. We might have reproached ourselves for allowing her to miss two years, which, let's face it, were not fully dedicated to the cello. But she actually managed to bridge the gap within three weeks and she is right back to the standard of her former class. On top of that, she now gives Latin lessons. Something else interesting transpired from all this: when one goes to school year in year out, boredom sets in, and the pressure becomes more evident than the advantages. But in this case, the interruption led Anita to realize that the state of vegetating was bad and she has thrown herself into her work with great energy and pleasure. I am surprised how easy she finds everything, and it would be excellent if she could still get her Abitur [the equivalent of 'A' levels]. But we don't want to make any plans at the moment. By the way, she also had a kind of improvised test from the first conductor of the Berlin Kulturbund, Rudolf Schwarz [the Kulturbund Deutscher Juden was a cultural association permitted by the authorities up to 1941] which she passed with flying colours ... Renate still looks very frail and is in need of recuperation after her tonsillitis [see page 39]. She has started her singing lessons again and her teacher thinks a lot of her.

When I have recovered somewhat from the strains of these last three months, I will consider giving my voice an overhaul before it becomes totally neglected.

... A short while ago a visit to uncle Edward [in America] became a possibility again. We are having a lively correspondence about this right now ... Take care, keep well and write again!

Many, many kisses,

Yours ...

I wrote:

January 1941

Dearest M,

I am writing to you in bed because I just have no time out of bed. You wouldn't believe how much I have got to do. Apart from school, where I have to go every afternoon and sometimes in the morning too, I have Auerbach (harmony) twice a week and I am *giving* Latin coaching lessons to three people, which brings in quite a considerable sum of money.

To cap all this, there is a concert here on Thursday in the Kulturbund where I will be playing a sonata.

The concert is going to be repeated no less than four times. Anyway, if I knew where I could buy time, I would be very happy. If you only realized how I envy all those people over there who have you with them! I can easily imagine you turning the whole place upside down with your cheeky face ... I kiss you a hundred thousand times from all my heart,

Yours, dead-tired Anita

My mother:

21st February 1941

My dearest beloved Jandel,

The day before yesterday your birthday letter for Grossfloh arrived. Only one week late ... She was very happy with it. She would have been happier still if she had been able to read it herself, but that is almost impossible even for younger eyes. Renate finally deciphered the letter and read it out ... You were telling us about your charges and how you were trying to infuse some culture into them. It is really good for us to know that you feel you have values within yourself which you want to convey to other people. You know how hurt I often used to feel when you shut yourself off from us and we started to become strangers in our innermost souls. How wonderful it would be if we could live together once more. I notice time and time again from your letters that things would be completely different now. We have closed ranks here ... Did I tell you that Edward has had his name engraved on a wall of fame along with 600 other chosen people? I am so glad that the rheumatism has gone. The enclosed photos were taken at Grossfloh's birthday party. I don't look quite as dreadful as I do in the picture ... For today, many thousands of kisses,

Yours Mu

My father:

7th March 1941

... Talking of the theatre and concerts, Tita appeared in public for the first time yesterday, not counting the school concerts. It was a great success. She got over her nerves a few days before. Her playing was absolutely confident and the applause was quite unanimous, especially among the really musical members of the audience. The concert will be repeated this week and she will feel even more confident, having become familiar with the acoustics of the hall. Much as we regret that Tita has had no real lessons for such a long time, I wouldn't wish her to be uprooted from school so soon again, now that she is doing so well. On the day of the concert she had just got her Latin work back. She came top, with another girl, which after a gap of two years must certainly mean something. She is also outstanding in drawing. If you were to see her perspective drawings your heart would rejoice, since this is also one of your special subjects. It all suggests that Anita is quite a girl. There is unfortunately a reverse side to the coin. Anita goes to bed very late these days ... I hope we will soon hear from you again via Vally [in Switzerland] ...

Ever yours

It is interesting that school, which was traditionally a most hated institution, turned into something like a haven – a focal point where you pursued such 'vitally important' things as Latin vocabulary when all around you the world was falling to pieces. Eventually the Jewish schools were closed (see page 39). But what will for ever stick in my mind is that, after that had happened, we found ourselves gathered in some teacher's private house as a matter of course, and lessons continued in a skeleton pursuit of learning.

Whilst I was back at school, Renate helped my father in the 'office' and took singing lessons. She wrote:

[April 1941]

Dearest M ...

Many happy returns! You are rapidly acquiring antiquity value! But you could scarcely get any wiser than you are already! If only we could have a really good quarrelling session again one day!! What do you think? Maybe it will not be *too* long now. Unthinkable!! Just for your information: I do not use make-up but only a little powder which gives my skin a peach-like appearance!! I am sure Kurt would not object, especially as the pimples have now gone. I am madly busy, partly in the household and partly as typist, since I do all the correspondence for Va now ... Apart from that, I am giving lessons and also taking some as well. My 'singing career' seems slightly out of place now but I enjoy it ...

That's all for today. I embrace you,

As always, your crazy Re

Forced labour

Meanwhile the hounding of the Jews grew steadily worse. My father was no longer working as a lawyer but, by special dispensation, he still represented a certain Count Künigl who had such a complicated lawsuit, which had been going on for so many years, that it would have been impossible for it to be taken on by any other lawyer. Count Künigl had obtained permission to be represented by my father, although he was a Jew, and he did his very best to help us later on. Mercifully this kept my father fully occupied till the end.

Of course ration cards had by now been issued: Jewish ones had a 'J' stamped on them, and shopping hours for Jews were restricted. The yellow star had been introduced. People were rounded up and disappeared; compulsory war-work was introduced; and it was a matter of luck whether you found yourself working on a rubbish tip, as my sister Renate had for a while. She had not lasted long on the tip as she became very ill:

January 1941

Dearest M,

Now I am seventeen years and one day old and I feel most peculiar. Unfortunately I had to spend that day being ill. It has quite a story attached to it: at the end of December I started some work during which I contracted an ugly throat infection. Then I got better and went out with the permission of the doctor. It was not long before I had a relapse. Now I am better again and will stay another two days at home ... [Renate is referring here to her work at the rubbish tip, where she had to sort out 'precious' items like toothpaste tubes and old tin cans from among dead rats, and such like. In fact she got so ill that she was provisionally exempted from having to do this work by the very authorities who had conscripted her.]

Hurry up and write, and take many greetings and kisses from

Yours Re

To return to April 1941, I wrote this:

April 1941

This is the second birthday on which I cannot congratulate you personally ... but the kisses and good wishes I am sending you are all the warmer ... I have now put four concerts behind me, and I have had reasonable success. Twice I even had to play an encore. Today we had the not so enchanting news that the High School is being disbanded within a few days. What that means either for the teachers or for the pupils cannot be completely assessed at the moment. So far we have no news about what will happen next ... The fate of our school is not unique ...

... We are now doing – or rather *were* doing – projection drawings at school (may it rest in peace). I enjoy this very much, and when Hadda looked at mine the other day, he told me it was my duty to be good at drawing because of you!

Up to now I have nearly always had an 'A' for my work ... We had a very nice afternoon in class the other day. We read Tolstoy's folk tales, *What People Live By*. (Do you know it?) And then we listened to records of *Death and the Maiden*, unbelievably beautifully played by the Busch Quartet. Do you ever have the opportunity to hear chamber music in the flesh? ... With the best will in the world I cannot think of anything worth writing about any more. Carry your second 'o' in honour [she had just become twenty], and once again, many happy returns,

Yours Anita

My father:

3rd July 1941

My dear Mariandel,

... I just want to let you know that we are all right, with the exception of Renate. The work she has to do at the moment is a terrible strain on her. We only hope that she will get over it ...

I have had a phone-call from Count K. He was on his way to us but had to turn back because of the new circumstances. He is hoping to get here in mid July. We have a great deal to discuss, especially since it has recently become very doubtful once again whether we will be able to pay uncle Edward our planned visit.

Many greetings,

Yours ...

Renate was transferred to a paper factory at Sacrau, where I later joined her.

17th July 1941

My dear little one,

I have had such a bad conscience that I hardly dare write to you. But I am now taking the opportunity of my birthday to do so at last. Please don't be cross. Today I am all of sixteen years old and my birthday presents were more than generous. I've had a wonderful *History of Art* and a German/Latin dictionary (which I wanted, and because of which more than one person has declared me mad), an historical atlas, *Music of the Nations* and *The Concert*. So much for the books. Also two blouses and a dress (manufacturer Mutti), flowers *en gros*, soap, a pair of socks, some sweets and music which I still have to buy. In the afternoon we played quartets ...

We had a lovely farewell party. Our class acted *The Broken Jug*. It was a great success. I was the Judge. We had amazing costumes, thanks of course to Hadda.

As far as I am concerned, I am just about to change *métier* again. On 1st August I shall start working in the hospital laboratory. I am very much looking forward to this, although I can't yet visualize what my attitude to the various appetizing excrements will be. But we shall see.

We were madly happy with your letter as ever ... I always show your letters to Mr Hadda who loves you dearly and sends his best regards. He really is such a nice man. (The job in the hospital is also thanks to him!)

I'll send you a photograph soon and ask you to do the same. I hope you haven't changed too much. I am really afraid of that. Well, dearest ... I kiss you countless times ...

Yours sixteen years old, Anita

This letter from my father is not dated but must have been written on 23rd October 1941:

My dear Mariandel,

Yesterday on my birthday we must have been thinking of each other. It was wonderful that we were still able to drink a cup of real coffee. The small birthday table became a little larger with some of the hopes which we put on it in our imagination. Mainly the hope that we will see you again soon. It's nearly two years now that we have been parted. In the meantime, you must have changed somewhat, and you would probably not recognize your sisters ... We are daily expecting news from Edward ... We often re-read the first letter from the Rev Fisher. When I said good-bye to Dr Beak, I had to promise to let him have a copy for his collection. He wrote to me saying that such a letter is a real antidote to the hate between men ... As soon as we have news from uncle Edward, we will write immediately! We heard that uncle H has had to move away recently. His letters sounded pretty desperate. We tried to cheer him up a bit.

... For today I just wanted to tell you that we finished my birthday with some exciting writing games. The children won most of the time, of course.

Many, many greetings and kisses,

Yours ...

October 1941

My dearest M,

... We hadn't been so happy for a long time as when we got your letters. We laughed till we cried ... If we were together now, we would having discussions about all sorts of things that are impossible to write about.

As to my – or rather *our* – occupation, you already know what we are doing from Renate's letter. I expect you basked in the thought that I had managed to get into the laboratory and that I am busily examining blood and sputum. Instead of this, I am now in fact in a paper factory and serve the multitude by providing toilet-rolls with labels. I have attained a dexterity at doing this which I'll probably never be able to reach on the cello. I'm sticking labels on about 5000 rolls daily, work in two shifts, 6-2 and 2-10, and have a journey of approximately one hour. Renate is working in a different department: napkins. This is considerably better but the hours are longer and she has to get up every morning (most Sundays included) at 4 a.m. while I always have a week [with the later shift] to catch up with my sleep. You must know from your cow-shed experience that getting up at 4 a.m. doesn't rank among the most outstanding pleasures. Especially in winter ...

I hope that we will soon have news from you again. This is one of our rare, real pleasures!!!

Thousands and thousands of kisses,

From yours, Anita

The factory was some distance outside the town. As we worked in those two long shifts, 6-2 and 2-10, it was impossible for us to get to the shops at the hours which were permitted for Jews. Furthermore, as the scale of pay was based on age, because of my extreme youth, I barely received enough to cover my fares. I became supremely adept, however, at sticking labels around toilet-rolls. Eventually I graduated to working the machines themselves and I must have turned out millions.

The work-force in the factory consisted of Jews, Poles and French prisoners of war. Since we spoke French and we only lived from day to day by some sort of dispensation, we soon made contact with the PoWs. It was of course strictly forbidden. We chose to ignore this and quickly got involved in all sorts of clandestine activities. In time we evolved a tremendous system of communication which was foolproof – or so it seemed at the time.

There were three toilets in a row. One for Jews, one for Poles and one for the odd German that worked there. On the other side of the wall from the toilets was the PoWs' refectory. Try to imagine an old-fashioned flushing system using a chain held in place by a sort of metal ring that was plugged into the wall, presumably to prevent it from being pulled in any old direction. We discovered that this ring was not firmly fixed into the wall and could easily be removed, leaving a hole about an inch in diameter that led straight into the refectory. It was something like the wall in *A Midsummer Night's Dream*.

This hole became a most convenient letterbox and was a more or less safe way of talking to a PoW: you put your mouth – or your ear, as the case may have been – close to the hole, and whispered whatever you had to say. It was totally inaudible in the adjoining toilets. We used the method successfully for a considerable time. We were so attuned to one another that all that was needed was for somebody to see me go to the toilet – which I must have done a lot more frequently than normal – and invariably a French prisoner would be there on the other side of the wall.

However, as time went by, we must have been observed more closely than we realized. One day, I found the famous hole plastered up, and that was the end of that ... Except that by then we had done most of our 'dirty' work, which consisted mainly of procuring civilian clothes and forging passes. Both Renate and I were able to write the German gothic script, and we still had a typewriter, which was all that was left from my father's thriving practice. The papers we produced were 'leave passes' for French civilian workers, of whom there were many in Germany at that time (as well as PoWs). The civilian workers were young men who had been rounded up by the Germans in France and sent to work in Germany. The 'official' stamp for these documents was furnished by other people, whose identity I did not know, but who were undoubtedly members of the French Resistance.

Many years after these events, I visited the Imperial War Museum in London where there was an exhibition of items used by Eric Williams of the celebrated 'Wooden Horse' escape, and to my great astonishment I discovered that Williams had used one of these very papers for *his* escape. I got in touch with him, and he was most intrigued by my story since he had been convinced that his papers had been supplied by MI9.

Our link with the French Resistance finally led to our own arrest in 1942. We were naturally aware of the fact that we were under suspicion of being involved with the French prisoners. The blocking of the hole in the lavatory wall was merely one indication.

A large number of prisoners had escaped from the Sacrau paper factory, and we had been meticulously watched by the Gestapo for quite a long time. We took the decision that we would attempt to make a run for it ourselves and try to reach the unoccupied zone of France. It was a desperate step and, needless to say, we did not succeed. We equipped ourselves with our own travel papers. My name on the papers was Madeleine Demontaigne, and my occupation 'worker in an upholstery factory'. We did not know whether there were really any female French civilian workers in Germany, but it was worth a try. We had absolutely nothing to lose. We did not get very far. Just as we were about to board the train

(from: Corsica)

c/o Collins, Publishers,
14 St. James's Place,
London S.W.1.

25th March 1974

Miss Anita Lasker-Wallfisch,
27 Chelmsford Square,
London NW10.

Dear Miss Wallfisch,

Many thanks for your letter of February 17th - which has only just been forwarded to me by Collins.

Your letter has shed some light on one aspect of my escape which has always been rather obscure to me. The paper you refer to is, I suppose, the travel document from the Metallhuttenwerke factory in Breslau? All the papers we used were supplied by the Escape Committee in Stalag-Luft III and their origin was kept intentionally vague in case we were re-captured. Since returning to England I have not enquired further as I have always assumed that the papers originated in M.I.9 in England.

I should be most interested to know more details. Were you employed by Metallhuttenwerke? I am fascinated by all aspects of escape and indeed have compiled three collections of other people's escape stories in addition to my own TUNNEL and WOODEN HORSE.

If there is anything else you can tell me - for instance about your connection with my own papers - please write C/O Collins, as I am sailing from Corsica in a few days and will be on the move all summer. (Collins send me a batch of mail whenever I can let them have a temporary address.)

I reciprocate your wishes for my good health and do hope that your terrible experiences in Auschwitz and Belsen did not impair your own.

Yours sincerely,

London, March 1974. Letter from Eric Williams who escaped from Stalag Luft III by means of the 'Wooden Horse' with travel documents we helped forge in Breslau at the main station in Breslau, which would take us out of Germany and into the unoccupied zone of France, we were arrested by the Gestapo.

But I am jumping ahead … While we were doing our stint at the factory, the dreaded day came. My aunt and uncle had already been deported, and on 9th April 1942 it was my parents' turn. They were not arrested in the street, but they were given twenty-four hours' notice to report at an assembly point.

My parents are deported

On 19th June 1945, two months after the liberation, I wrote a long letter to Marianne telling her about these traumatic last hours with our parents. Here is the relevant passage in this letter:

Belsen Camp, 19th June 1945

My best, one and only …

… I would like to tell you a little about the 'departure' of our parents. We knew the day before that it was going to catch up with them. Mutti cried a great deal – she must have felt instinctively that the end was now coming and that she was seeing us for the last time. We had just had another letter from you via Switzerland. Mutti treasured this letter like the apple of her eye, and it made her very happy. Now I must tell you that, had we tried with all our might to go with them, we would probably have succeeded. *Our* names were not on the list but if we had simply presented ourselves, it is unlikely that we would have been sent back. However, Vati – our clever Vati - wouldn't hear of it. 'It is better for you to stay. Where we are going, you get there soon enough.' We didn't exchange many words. There was a lot to do – packing – packing … (We were not aware then that everything was going to be taken off them anyway.) Vati concentrated on concluding his own – or rather everyone else's – affairs [among other things, he completed the Vermögenserklärung, or declaration of possessions: see Appendix 1 on page 146]. It would not have been our Vati if he had just abandoned everything. So he worked late into the night typing and dictating. Renate meanwhile went to bed because even excitement tires you out. Vati asked me to wait for him. I took a notebook and pencil and sat waiting with Mutti next door. She cried and cried. Our poor, poor dear lovely Mutti, she was so frightened. The only consolation for me is that wherever it was they went, they were together, because Vati wrote us three letters before the news from them came to an end. Vati had the strength of a hero, and maybe Mutti was able to draw on it. Vati wrote nothing factual in those letters, nothing about what was happening. At the very end he said: *send food*. That he wrote nothing more detailed is proof that things were bad. We assumed that our parents were together then since Vati wrote: 'Mutti cannot add anything to this letter because she is not feeling well; she is ill.' And in his last letter there was just a psalm: 'I will lift up mine eyes unto the hills from whence cometh my help.' I often thought of this when things were really bad for me.

I will go back again now. I waited with Mutti for Vati. At 2 a.m. he finally came and called me. Vati had aged twenty years that night. He dictated everything I had to do into my book – how to pay the rent and the gas bill, whom I had to write to – and he gave me power of attorney to sign his name if ever a signature should be required. 'I count on you Anita' (you know that Vati did not easily count on anybody). By the way, I will mention that I think I coped well with all the technicalities. I did have a lot of trouble with the Inland Revenue people, who pursued us relentlessly, right into prison. All this is now over and done with. I am aware of the fact that on the night of 8th to 9th April I took on responsibility not only for the rent and the gas, but for something much bigger. Especially because Renate was asleep at the time and I was alone. Do you fully understand? That night was decisive for me, although I only became conscious of its real significance much later. Yes, we should never cease to be thankful to our parents and we must live as though they can always see us …

The rest of the letter will be given when we reach 1945 (see page 114).

Had we really wanted to go with our parents, and just turned up at the assembly point, I dare say nobody would have sent us back home, as I have said. Even if making toilet paper was a 'reserved occupation' at the time. But it was my father who decided that we should not *corriger la fortune*, and should remain where we were. What the decision must have cost him is too awful to contemplate, and I only began to appreciate his predicament when I became a parent myself.

Had my father not followed his instinct, or whatever you want to call it, I would not be sitting here writing this. Our parents were sent to a place called Izbica, near Lublin. I went to the Wiener Library after the war. This library is named after its founder who was called Dr Alfred

Wiener. It is in London and contains comprehensive documentation on the persecution of the Jews. There I found evidence of the fate of this and similar transports. At Isbica people had to dig their own graves and undress, and then they were shot into the graves.

It will, I am sure, be understandable if I rarely let my imagination dwell on the way my parents were put to death.

I would merely like to mention something here that I did not tell my sister about when I recounted these terrible last hours. It may seem very trivial, but I remember it vividly. My father's final words to me were: 'Please watch your walk.' The reason he said this was that I am pigeon-toed, and he always deplored this lack of gracefulness in me.

At the moment when all this happened, it was so inevitable that Renate and I went about our business as usual when we got home, maybe with that much grimmer a determination to try and beat the system. We still had a glimmer of hope that our parents would be released at the last minute from the transport because Count Künigl was an influential man, and we had tried to alert him to the fact that my parents were to be deported. He told us later what precisely he did try and do. He went to the Gestapo and *demanded* that my father be released because he needed him. He was told that if my father's name had not yet been registered, they would let him go. We managed to piece the story together because I had the two messages my father had miraculously managed to get to us. The first one was that he was reasonably confident he would be released because my mother's and his name had been called out for registration almost immediately after they entered the assembly point, long before any other names were called. But he waited in vain for his release ... What in fact must have happened is that after registering my father at once they were then able to tell Count Künigl 'with a clear conscience' that they had tried to release him but that, alas, it was too late.

The last message we received from my father was on a postcard. God knows how he managed to smuggle it out. All it contained was the quotation from the psalm, and the PS that my mother was unable to add anything because she was not well ...

That is all I am left with as far as my parents are concerned.

To think that thirty-five years later my sister should have been threatened with legal proceedings because she had had occasion to speak on German television about the fate of her parents, and had been promptly accused of 'defaming the reputation of the SS'.

3

Alone in Breslau with Renate

We were left alone to battle on. And it was a battle.

My parents had gone, and so too had my aunt and uncle in whose apartment we were living. My grandmother, who had later moved in as well, was still with us. She was eighty-two, as I said earlier, and incapable of understanding, or else unwilling to understand, what was going on around her. We continued working in the paper factory, and the problem of getting hold of food, with the restricted shopping hours for Jews, was virtually insurmountable. We got some relief by stealing 'travel food coupons', which had found their way to the factory for recycling. These coupons were undated and had no information on them about whom they belonged to. Most important of all, there was no 'J' for Jew printed on them, and they could be used in any shop since they were supposed to be for people who were away from home. It was a dangerous activity stealing and using these coupons, but that is what we did, and it helped a bit. Renate usually did the shopping, since she does not look as Jewish as I do.

I wrote this letter to my relatives in Switzerland:

Breslau, 2nd July 1942

Dear Tante Vally and Onkel Siegfried,

Thank you so much for the little parcels which reached us a few days ago, and which are more than welcome. Unfortunately we can only reply by letter to your telegram. Our health is not very good and the constant worry about our parents, from whom we have no news, weighs heavily on us. Grossmama is still living here. She is fairly well; only you can imagine that looking after her as well as an old couple who are living with us (so that we are able to survive) is very difficult, on top of our work ... I hope that we shall have more news from you soon because this is the only thing that makes us feel that we are not totally alone. Please give Marianne our love, and greetings to you ...

Yours Anita

Next on the list for deportation was my grandmother, and I remember getting her ready and hanging a bag around her neck with all the various medications in it that she was supposed to take. She did not really understand what was happening to her – thank God – and she retained her pride and dignity to the end. I took her to the assembly point (this time it was a school yard), and stood by her side until her name was called for registration; and I was treated to a most impressive spectacle by this proud old lady. A Gestapo man sat at a table reading out names, and the people who were called had to walk past the table to the other side of the yard. When he called 'Lasker', my grandmother walked past the table, but not without stopping in front of the Gestapo man. She looked him straight in the face, and said very loudly: '*Frau* Lasker to you'. I thought he would hit her there and then, but not a bit of it. He just said simply: '*Frau* Lasker'. I was extremely proud of her as she passed him unmolested. An object lesson in the treatment of bullies.

Now Renate and I were the only occupants left in our flat. The rooms which had been vacated by my aunt and uncle, my mother and father, and finally my grandmother – and the old couple – had all been sealed by the Gestapo (see Appendices 1 and 2 on pages 146 and 149), and Renate and I lived in a sort of limbo with no one to care for us, and no one to care for. Obviously this state of affairs could not last for ever. There was still the skeleton of a Jewish community remaining in Breslau, and since we were very much minors, we soon had a guardian assigned to us. I remember we gave this guardian a hard time. Rumours had spread about our behaviour and activities in the factory, which most certainly did not conform to the general passivity of those few people who had so far escaped deportation.

It was strongly suggested that we should be moved to an orphanage. We did not much like the idea, as we thought it would cramp our style. But eventually this is exactly what happened.

Breslau, 6th September 1942

Dear Onkel Siegfried and Tante Vally,

I have just received your card and want to reply immediately. Tomorrow we are moving out of the flat to an orphanage because we have been left completely alone. Grossmama and the other couple who lived with us have also gone away now. We still have no news from our parents. Have you been in touch with the Red Cross? Have you had any news from

Marianne? … Our new address is: Waisenhaus [the Orphanage], Wall Strasse 9 … Our work is very strenuous and the persistent heat is unbearable. We are glad that you are well. Renate is cooking at the moment and sends her regards.

Yours Anita

PS Tante Lucie has also gone.

This letter was sent on by Siegfried and Vally to their son Harry Goldschmidt, who – as I discovered after the war – had some contacts near the border and evolved an ingenious if totally unrealistic plan for smuggling us across the frontier into Switzerland …

Dear Harry, I have just received this. Please phone if I can do anything and tell me what it might be. It seems that letters to Jews are not delivered, or would your contact not have sent it? I gather that the Jewish people who are working are being put into a youth hostel where of course they will be watched much more closely than at the Höfchenstrasse [our address before we went to the orphanage].

Greetings … Mama

Once we got to the orphanage, we could no longer understand why we had fought so much against it. It was such a relief to be cared for again all of a sudden, and to have a plate of food put in front of us without having to go through an abysmal struggle to obtain it.

The big problem was how to effect our 'great escape' without (a) giving the game away in the orphanage, and (b) involving anybody in 'complicity' which could have dire consequences for them.

We overcame the first problem by pretending to go to work as usual at some ridiculous hour in the morning on the day we had planned for our escape. The second problem we failed to resolve, and the result was even more disastrous than we anticipated. That day, instead of going to work, we went straight to the house of some friends. They were a mixed-marriage couple. The husband was Aryan and the wife Jewish. That was a permissible combination in those days. God knows why, but it was more permissible than the other way round. We spent the day there until it was time for us to go to the station to catch our train. It was appallingly hard to say goodbye. The future was such a menacing enigma. Our friends, Werner and Ruth Krumme, wanted to accompany us. We begged them not to, and we should have *forbidden* it. They were both to be arrested with us on the station platform.

Werner, the Aryan, eventually became a prominent prisoner in Auschwitz who made it his business to help as many people as possible. He survived the camp and the war, and died a few years ago. A tree has been planted in his memory in Yad Va'shem, the Memorial to the Holocaust in Israel. So well deserved! Ruth, his Jewish wife, died in Auschwitz shortly after her arrival. The fate of these wonderful people has weighed heavily on me as I seemed to be directly responsible for what happened.

There we were, at the main station in Breslau, on the platform for the train to Paris. The whole thing was like a bad dream. Naturally we were frightened. After all, we only had the vaguest idea what would happen to us once we arrived in Paris, among other things. I carried with me a notebook with the addresses of several contacts in France, should we ever get that far. That was all. We did not think too far ahead. Getting away from Germany was all that concerned us at the time.

We stowed our cases on the train. Renate was inside the carriage and I was on the platform talking to our friends. That was when it happened. Several men in civilian clothes approached, and I heard the fateful word 'Gestapo'. My friends and I were arrested. I had a crazy, fleeting thought that perhaps they didn't know about Renate, and that if she stayed in the carriage long enough, she might get away. But no such luck. She appeared at the door and joined the party.

We found out subsequently that the Gestapo had had tabs on us for some time and known our every move for months, as I have mentioned. We were marched off to the Railway Police Station. As we sat there waiting endlessly, we had ample time to contemplate our hopeless situation. It was then that I thought of the cyanide I had hidden in my stocking.

I must explain that before our arrest, when we were still 'free', it was the fashion to carry cyanide on one's person, as ultimately no one could reasonably expect to escape arrest by the Gestapo. It had a comforting effect and gave you a choice. You did not *have* to go through with possible torture by the Gestapo. You could decide to put an end to it all. So during the period when I was working at the factory, producing and labelling toilet-rolls, forging documents for French PoWs and preparing my own escape, I carried with me a little glass bottle containing cyanide. It had been given to me by my good friend Konrad, who had access to this sort of amenity. For reasons best known to himself, he asked me one day to return the poison to him until I was ready to embark on my escape. This

I did, and he duly gave it back to me as he had promised. When the cyanide was in my possession for the first time, I had opened the bottle to take a whiff of the bitter-almonds smell.

While we sat waiting for God knows what, it occurred to me that this was precisely the situation for which we had equipped ourselves with the cyanide. The prospect of actually taking it, however, was not too appealing. After a whispered argument we decided that it would be foolish to wait. I extracted the stuff from my stocking, divided it into two equal parts (all this took place under the table where we were sitting), and it merely remained for us to find a suitable moment. It came when the car which was to take us to the Gestapo Headquarters failed to turn up, and it was decided that we should walk the short distance. There was a complete blackout at that point, and off we walked, Renate and I, and all the other people who had been arrested with us, encircled by the Gestapo and their dogs. As I said, neither of us was madly sold on the idea of taking the poison, and we certainly did not want to die at different times. We decided to count up to three and … go. This we did, at the corner of Garten Strasse and Schweidnitzer Strasse, as they were then called. (I revisited the spot some years ago.) As my tongue touched the white powder, I imagined I was dying and I remember that I felt very faint. But lo and behold, I was not dying but still marching along. The taste in my mouth was sweet and not bitter-almondy as I had expected.

For my friend Konrad, guided by great wisdom, had substituted icing-sugar for the cyanide during the brief period in which he had taken back the little bottle. Our relief at still being alive was enormous, although we were now heading straight for the Gestapo Building, and into an unknown but without doubt extremely unpleasant future that we could imagine only too vividly.

I met my friend again after the war. He came to see me at the Lüneburg Trial, where I was a witness (see Appendix 4 on page 157). I thanked him for the icing-sugar! The episode proves – if nothing else – our total ignorance of what the next moment may hold in store for us. Except that in normal life the circumstances might have been rather less extreme.

4

Convicted Criminals

With no way of escape, and since we now clearly had to face the music, we decided to make one last desperate attempt to save the situation by remaining 'French' for the time being, and we had the 'chutzpah', the outrageous audacity, to demand an interpreter. It was pretty farcical. An interpreter was provided, and we were questioned about our personal data. All in French.

When it was over, we sat around a little longer, this time waiting to be taken to the Graupe, which is the nickname for the prison in Breslau. It is a huge red-brick building in the middle of the town, around the corner from the Gestapo Building, in Graupen Strasse. I still had on me the small notebook containing the names of my contacts in France. I knew I had to get rid of it somehow. Looking back, I have come to the conclusion that the people who were dealing with us were inordinately stupid, because I managed to get rid of the incriminating evidence without much difficulty. I asked to be allowed to go to the lavatory where I tore the notebook into little pieces and flushed it down. It was all too easy and I was most relieved. I think that in such a dire situation a kind of amnesia takes over and one copes with life literally five minutes at a time. It may sound rather like a television thriller, but everything took place exactly as I am telling it.

It was late at night when we were eventually taken to the prison. There we were properly 'processed' and, luckily for us, the Gestapo showed their total incompetence once again because they did not instruct the prison staff to put us into separate cells. That meant that we had all night to plan how we would handle the Gestapo interrogation we were expecting the next morning.

The prison staff were not particularly objectionable as far as I can recall. We were still pretending to be French; and we took the obligatory bath and were issued with prison clothes. The guards trotted out their school French and probably found us light relief from the daily routine. We were then put into a cell, and I think it was only when we heard the key turn behind us that it came home to us what had happened.

The inside of a prison is just as you might imagine it from those television films.

The most striking features are the echoes and the never-ending sound of jangling keys. The cells were small and intended for *one* person, not *four*, the number of people in ours. Conditions were pretty rough. In those days there were no outings to lavatories. There was simply a Kübel in one corner of the cell. It did have a lid, but that is the only thing one could say in its favour. A Kübel was a sort of bucket which rested on a wooden construction. One of the many lunatic rules in prison was that you had to keep this Kübel gleaming with the aid of Schammot. This is some sort of sandy, gritty substance which had to be rubbed into the surface. The process made a dreadful scraping sound and it was a deeply distasteful occupation. The same treatment had to be applied to the tiny metal washbasin, and God help you if these items did not shine like silver. There was only one bed in the cell, and the rest of the inmates had to sleep on mattresses on the floor, which had to be tidied away during the day.

The first day in prison was quite terrible, and I could not see how I was going to be able to stand it. Although we had scarcely been free agents before our arrest, hearing a key turned behind you and being locked into a small cell is a devastating experience. The hours dragged by and we were faced with hunger for the first time. At least we were together. Apart from the comfort of not being entirely alone, there was another most important aspect of our being together: as I have said, we had time and opportunity to make plans.

Several days passed and we were not called. We were just miserably unhappy and frightened. As we reflected on our hopeless situation, we realized that we could not keep on posing as French girls for ever. We knew that the disappearance of two Jewish girls in a middle-sized town in war-time could not have gone unnoticed and must have been linked to us. I learned later that in fact our disappearance became notorious and that a brave priest had said prayers for us during a church service.

We decided to come clean about our real identity. We asked to see the prison Governor, who turned out to be a highly intelligent and civilized lady. I had dealings with her later on which I shall talk about. We went to see her and admitted that we were not French but plain Jewish girls by the name of Renate and Anita Lasker, and not Demontaigne. She took it fairly well, as far as I can recollect.

The unpleasantness started when we had to go down to the office to register. The very guards who had tried so hard to speak French to us suddenly realized what fools they had made of themselves and they were furious. I mainly remember a certain Frau Nau. She was fairly high-ranking in the prison service, and obviously brainwashed by the system, unlike the Governor who, by her reactions to our confession, made it patently clear that she was not a Nazi. Frau Nau was a different kettle of fish. When she heard that Renate and I were just two Jewish girls, she came to see us in our cell and embarked on a long lecture in an absurd, pseudo-motherly tone and proceeded to explain to us that we absolutely *had* to realize that Hitler was the wisest man in the world and understand that the Jews *had* to be destroyed. She almost pleaded with us to accept that simple fact. It was such a ridiculous conversation that Renate and I had a job not to burst out laughing. Thank God we managed to preserve a sense of humour in the face of so much undiluted stupidity. When the débâcle of Stalingrad was taking place (part of the German army was trapped there, and the campaign probably marked the beginning of the end for the Germans), this same lady declared that Hitler knew precisely what he was doing and that the encirclement of the German army in Stalingrad was a cleverly disguised plan of Hitler's. Everything was going very well indeed, and on no account did we have any reason to rejoice ... I can hear her voice now; and as a matter of fact we later amused ourselves by imitating her propaganda speeches. I became expert at impersonating her, and was once caught in the act by another guard. I think she must have found it funny too, because I got away with it unpunished.

Now that our real identity was established, we were transferred to the *Jewish* cell. It would be unthinkable to mix clean Aryan criminals with dirty Jews. In this way we rejoined Ruth Krumme, our dear friend who had accompanied us to the station and been arrested for this crime. Apart from the three of us, there was also an old lady there from Czechoslovakia. I don't remember her crime, but merely that it was not easy to endure her. We were unbelievably cramped, and she was the senior citizen so to speak.

We still had not been summoned by the Gestapo, but by now we had evolved a plan of campaign. We decided that we had to lie as much as possible, and give away as little as possible. How to do so successfully was a serious problem since not only is it difficult to lie but it is doubly diffi-cult for two people to lie simultaneously without contradicting each other on small points.

At this juncture we did not know how much of our clandestine activity was known to the Gestapo. We hit upon the idea that the easiest way out of our dilemma would be for Renate, the older of the two of us, to do all the talking and answering of questions while I pretended that I knew hardly anything about anything, that I was just the little sister. I was under no circumstances to go into any matter in detail. In this way we thought we might have some chance of eliminating contradictions. Armed with our plan we sat and waited, scared and at the same time anxious to get it all over and done with.

While we waited and waited – the only thing one seems to do in prison – we had ample opportunity to acquaint ourselves with prison life. In those days there was no preoccupation with the 'well being' of prisoners. You were in prison, and there you stayed. No outings to the lavatory. You sat – slept – and relieved yourself in your cell.

The stench was disgusting since everything was multiplied by four. We left the cell once a day for half an hour to walk in a circle around the courtyard. Needless to say, speaking to other prisoners was strictly forbidden. There were the usual 'trusties' who dished out the food. It was insufficient and we suffered from severe hunger. It was also laced with bromide, which you could taste. But the worst memories I have of prison are concentrated in the first few days: that sound of the key turning behind you, above all. I also remember our total bewilderment, mixed with fear for the future, and a feeling of complete isolation and of time standing still.

It never ceases to amaze me that the human species is capable of adjusting to almost anything. Even when you are locked into a small stinking cell, suffering hunger and acute discomfort, a sort of routine emerges, which you start to live by. Your horizon merely contracts. Although I thought at first that I could never survive prison life, in fact I stood it extremely well. What is more to the point, later on, when I became a concentration camp dweller, I was to look back on my time in prison as I would today on a very enjoyable holiday.

At last we were called down and led to our first Gestapo interrogation. As well as being frightened, we also felt a certain relief. What we feared most had finally happened. There are certain features of this initial interrogation that stick in my mind vividly, probably because they were so unexpected.

The first thing we were asked to do was to identify and sign for our suitcases. Not a word was said about our sudden ability to speak German. The suitcases were lined up in front of us, and it transpired that one of them was missing. It was the one that Renate had stowed on the rack in our carriage since she had already got onto the train when I was arrested on the platform. I was not unduly perturbed by the missing suitcase since I did not anticipate needing any of its contents again, but the Gestapo were thrown out by such an obvious lapse of order. After all, 'Ordnung muss sein', order is order. We had to describe the colour and the contents of the case, and all was duly noted down and signed for by us. Quite ludicrous when you consider that the Gestapo were engaged in wholesale theft and murder.

We forgot about the case in time, and you can imagine my surprise when about a year later I was called to identify a suitcase that had just arrived. It was difficult to believe but there it was. An unlocked and unlabelled suitcase had travelled in war-time Germany on a train to Paris, and had been traced, identified and returned to its owner, who was an inmate of Breslau prison, and for whose life no one would have given tuppence. Everything was intact as far as I can recollect, and nothing was missing.

I found it hilariously funny. I signed for it knowing perfectly well that that was the last I would ever see of it. As it happens, I was wrong. I did see some of my clothes again, but they were being worn by one of the 'screws'. (I shall come back to this.) It made the whole thing even more remarkable.

Soon after identifying our belongings to the Gestapo, we were summoned once more, this time for the interrogation proper. Renate was called first, and to our astonishment she was returned to our cell before I was called the next day. So we had time to confirm our original plan. I performed my role pretending that I was hardly able to count up to three, that I had no idea what was going on, and that I always did what my big sister told me. It may not sound very nice now that I put it down on paper, but you must not forget that we were doomed people, and that all we could do was make some frantic and no doubt futile attempt to delay the final moment. We were improvising.

In the meantime we had a new arrival in our cell. Her name was Hanni-Rose Herzberg. She was a schoolfriend of ours. Her particular crime was that she had shared a room with us at the orphanage. She was arrested a few days after we had been, and it was through her that we knew about the impact our 'disappearance' had had on the outside world. It was like attending your own funeral. It gave us a great morale boost to learn about the priest who had had the courage to pray for us at a church service.

You will, I am sure, wonder why I say so little about the Gestapo interrogation. The truth is that I do not remember much about it. No doubt I was numb with fear. Neither Renate nor I were subjected to any particular torture, and the reason for this will become plain.

After twenty-one days in prison we knew that we were going to have a trial. This was good news indeed. The background was as follows. The Gestapo and the old-established system of law did not always see eye to eye with regard to the methods that were applied in dealing with 'crimes', which is scarcely surprising. There always seemed to be a period of twenty-one days during which the decision was taken whether you remained in the hands of the Gestapo, which meant immediate removal to a concentration camp, or the Law Courts took over, in which case you had a trial, of sorts. It goes without saying that it was most desirable to get out of the clutches of the Gestapo, even for a limited period. Time was of the essence. Every day *not* spent in a concentration camp was a day gained. Prison is not the most wonderful place to be, but nobody murders you there.

I am pretty certain that somewhere along the line an ex-colleague of my father's (who had been a well-known lawyer) had intervened on our behalf so that we were able to stay in prison and wait for our trial. It was an important respite. We had been arrested on 16th September, and the trial actually took place on 5th June the following year.

We had plenty of time to get used to being in prison. The thing around which our lives revolved was the big clock on the prison tower, which we were able to see if we craned our necks for a view out of the tiny window, high up in the wall. I must have looked at that clock a thousand times a day. Time really did seem to stand still. I don't know why I wanted time to pass. I dare say that it was mainly because we were hungry and always waiting for the next 'meal'. Meals were brought round by people called Kalfaktors and you were at their mercy. If they chose, they did not stir the soup in the cauldron, and that meant that you got little more than water. This problem took on major significance. Thank God that, as soon as it was evident we were going to remain in prison for a time, we were given some work to do.

The old lady in our cell had to sew buttons onto cardboard: an exceptionally boring job. We were given slightly superior work. We painted toy soldiers. It was probably because we had younger eyes. There was never enough daylight in the cell, and we had to work under a bare light bulb. It was a painstaking job. When you next see a toy soldier, take a closer look. There is a lot of detail there, like buttons which had to be carefully painted; but you could get a certain amount of satisfaction from trying to do it well. It helped while away the time that hung so heavily in the air.

Through painting these soldiers I made my first acquaintance with the British uniform: English bearskins and Scottish kilts. I found it fascinating. I also came to understand why the painting of toy soldiers is done by prisoners. If the work that goes into it was paid properly, nobody would be able to afford them.

It was a strain on our eyes because of the bare bulb and all those hours of staring at our work. I cannot tell you now how I managed to do this, but I got hold of some tissue paper, painted some green leaves on it and made it into a lampshade. This created a minor revolution. Nothing like it had ever been seen in a prison cell before, and the 'case' had to go to the highest authority for approval before I was allowed to keep the lampshade. It helped give our cell a more homely atmosphere.

The materials for producing the soldiers were supplied to us by a young girl who played an important role for me. Her name was Miss Neubert, and we called her Püppchen (Dolly) because she was very petite. She did not belong to the prison staff but was employed by the manufacturers of the soldiers, and wore civilian clothes. I regret very much that I never had occasion to speak to her again after the war and I would like to thank her for the moral support she gave me.

At first she just breezed in and out of the cell, collecting the soldiers that were ready and supplying the paints for a new batch with explanations about the colours we had to use. I think it was only after Renate had left our cell that she started talking and asking tentative questions. It soon developed into a routine. She would open the cell door and ask very loudly what we needed for the benefit of any guard who might be standing nearby. She would then partly close the door and continue the conversation in a soft voice. I would sometimes find bread, and once even a cake, that her mother had baked for us, in the bottoms of the cardboard boxes containing the unpainted soldiers. It is difficult to convey what this meant to me. It was a ray of sunshine. Her final, unforgettable contribution to my morale was when she came to see me on the day before my transfer to Auschwitz. I was no longer in my usual cell, and she must have made inquiries about where I was. She came into my cell, where I was on my own awaiting transportation. She brought me food and a collection of proverbs which she said her mother sent me with her best wishes.

It was typically German, and frightfully naïve, but so well meant. She clearly wanted to express her disgust at what was happening. It gave me a great lift at a time when I needed it most. The chats we had when I was painting soldiers were not particularly philosophical. We just gossiped, and it was probably through her that a small scandal broke out. That brings me back to the suitcase with my personal belongings which had rejoined me in prison after its lonely journey to Paris and back, and had been residing in the prison store-room.

One day, as we filed past the guards on our way to the courtyard for our daily exercise – when we walked silently in a circle – I noticed that one of the guards was wearing a dress that seemed familiar. I must explain here that not all the prison guards were dressed in uniform. I assume it was a war-time measure that some of them were civilians and wore civilian clothes. On my way back to the cell I made a point of verifying my first impression and of passing the guard in question as closely as I possibly could. I scrutinized her dress once more. I was not mistaken. She was wearing a dress that had been *my* dress. My mother used to make my dresses and there was no possibility that I was wrong. I can remember what it was like. It had a high collar and a pleated skirt, specially made for playing the cello. However, before I could be *absolutely* sure of the facts, I observed the guard for several days. I then recognized other items of clothing that had belonged to me. It was a unique situation: a prisoner finding that her guard is a thief. What had happened was that my renowned suitcase had been raided by the prison guard – who shamelessly paraded the stolen goods in front of our eyes. Perhaps this guard was not even aware of who the rightful owner was. It does not alter the morality of it. I told Miss Neubert, alias Dolly, about it all and, prisons being a micro-cosm where gossip flies around like wildfire, it took no time for the story to reach the Governor. I have mentioned that she was a distinguished lady and extremely correct. I was summoned to her office. She questioned me about my allegations, and I told her the simple truth. Namely that one of the guards was walking about in my clothes. It put her in an awkward position. A prisoner, and a Jew to boot, was accusing a guard of stealing. She could not merely ignore the matter since the prison was humming with the story. It was patently obvious that she believed me, but how could she be seen to believe a Jew, who was automatically a criminal and a liar, accusing a German guard of theft? (I was secretly interested in the possibility of collecting an additional prison sentence for 'wrongly accusing a German woman', knowing full well that more time in prison was preferable to existence in a concentration camp, where I would be ending up ultimately.) The Governor made it plain she was anxious for me to drop the whole thing so that it could be forgotten. She actually said that I must surely realize that the word of a Jew, however trustworthy *she* might think it was, weighed nothing against the word of a German. The interview ended and I was left with the satisfaction of knowing that the Governor at least knew my allegations were true. However, in Nazi Germany it was pointless pursuing such a matter.

Meanwhile life went on. We were hungry; we developed callouses on our bottoms; and we were learning to interpret the noises in the prison, and grasp the significance of being called down on a Monday, or a Thursday. We got to know which days transports went where, and found out more about our fellow prisoners, although talking to anybody was forbidden. We discovered that the pretty Czech girl in the cell opposite us was counting on getting a death sentence for sabotage.

We also heard on the grapevine that the Allies had landed in Sicily. I can no longer recall who told us about it, but it was the cause of much rejoicing. I was so happy and so hopeful that the nightmare might come to an end that I grabbed a box of buttons belonging to the old lady in the cell and threw them in the air, spilling hundreds and hundreds of them on the floor. We had it all worked out: if the Allies were in Sicily, it would only take them a few weeks to reach the prison in Breslau, and we would all be free. We were very happy for a very short time. As I bent down to pick up the buttons, which took a lot longer than spilling them, the sobering thought came to me that it just might take the Allies a little longer than that to reach us, and that they might not even get to us in time.

We sat there painting soldiers and looking at the clock a thousand times a day. (When I revisited Breslau a few years ago, I said 'hello' to this clock.) The future was unpromising. The present was clouded by uncertainty, and menacing.

Our next hurdle was the trial.

We were going to be tried by the Sondergericht, a special court, and I think this word was apt. The court was certainly 'special'. We were given the option of legal representation, which, as you would expect, was a charade. Nobody could really have defended us even if they had wanted to. What is more, it really was in our interest – absurd though it may

Paris, October 1946. Médaille de la Reconnaissance Française awarded to Renate and myself by the French Government

sound – to get as long a sentence as possible. If by some chance the court were to find us 'not guilty', and we were released from prison, we would never walk out free. We would be instantly rearrested by the Gestapo. But there was no danger of our being found not guilty. Our indictment was for three crimes: 'forgery', 'aiding the enemy', and 'attempted escape'.

If you analyse these alleged crimes, you will agree that the second two were laughable. *Their* enemy was not *our* enemy, and to attempt to escape certain death seems a curious criminal offence. (Incidentally, we were both awarded a medal by the French Government after the war: 'La Médaille de la Reconnaissance Française'.)

My memory of the trial is hazy. I was surprised to find so many of us sitting in the dock: everybody in fact who was in any way connected with us personally, or with the fabrication of the forged documents. Renate remembered the occasion better than I did, and I will include a piece here that she wrote some years ago about the trial and her subsequent departure to the penitentiary, the Zuchthaus, in Jauer:

Trial and arrival in Jauer
On the morning of our trial, Anita and I were completely calm, not because we had any hope that we might get away with a light sentence, but because we were both sure that there was no possible chance of our being acquitted or let off lightly. The German authorities still made a pretence of respecting legal traditions at that time. We were therefore allowed to appear in court in our civilian clothes. I remember that I insisted on wearing a dress of beige angora wool which my mother had embroidered in pretty colours and, being all of seventeen years old, I had illusions that I might impress our judges favourably by being dressed in a manner I then considered elegant. The trial turned out to be a farce, our appointed lawyer not even taking the trouble to be present during the procedure. Now I know, of course, that he did not appear because he was afraid to defend two Jewish girls who, in the eyes of the law, had committed the unforgivable sin of trying to escape from a life that was doomed to end in a concentration camp.

With us in the dock were two other Jews. My parents' friend Ruth Krumme, who was married to a German non-Jew and who had been arrested with her husband at the railway station in our town when they took us to the train in which my sister and I had hoped to escape to the then unoccupied zone of France, and a schoolfriend who had shared our room after my parents had been taken by the Gestapo. Her name was Hanni-Rose Herzberg, and she was the only daughter of a prosperous wine-merchant in Breslau. She was an extremely pretty girl with long blond hair and enormous brown eyes. Her only crime was that she happened to live with us. She had been arrested shortly after we had, and for many months we shared a prison cell with her. She had always been spoilt as a child and was therefore badly equipped to deal with the hardships of prison life. Hanni-Rose promptly fell ill soon after her arrest and spent many weeks in the prison hospital. On the day of the trial she was well again but very pale and frail. When the sentences were pronounced they held no real surprises. My sister was sentenced to spend eighteen more months in prison. I, as the older sister who was considered to be more responsible for my actions, got a sentence of three and a half years' hard labour. Both our friends, Ruth Krumme and Hanni-Rose Herzberg, were acquitted, which at that period meant immediate transfer to a concentration camp. A devilish irony. After hearing of their acquittal, and hoping that they might go free, the defendants were led out of the courtroom and immediately taken into custody by the Gestapo. We later learned that Ruth Krumme was sent to Auschwitz with the express recommendation that she should be killed on arrival, thus ridding her husband, who was a non-Jew, of the burden of a Jewish wife. Hanni-Rose also went to Auschwitz where she only survived for a few weeks.

My sister and I were relieved to be sentenced to further custody, hoping that our eventual transfer to a concentration camp would be delayed as much as possible and that maybe the war would end before that. Idle hopes they turned out to be. But it was such fantasies that kept us going. We were driven back to prison, catching a glimpse of our home town through the tiny heavily barred windows of the prison van. Two days later, came the ominous stereotyped call – known and feared by every prisoner: 'Renate Sara Lasker mit allen Sachen', meaning that I had to get ready immediately with my cell-gear in order to be transferred to the place where I was sentenced to spend the next three and a half years.

Even after forty years I find it difficult to describe my feelings when I had to say goodbye to my sister Anita. Although we were children, we both felt that this might be the last time we would see and hold each other. Our farewell was mercifully cut short by the prison guard who hurried me out of the cell. Downstairs I was duly processed, given back my civilian clothes, my suitcase and an envelope with the money I had been carrying when I was arrested the year before. I was driven in the now familiar prison van to the railway station and there I was locked up in a cramped room till the train arrived. In Germany at that time every train had two compartments specially reserved for prisoners, as the authorities did not want to risk encounters between their charges and ordinary civilian passengers.

The journey to the small town of Jauer was uneventful. I managed to see a little of the countryside through the windows, but I was not really interested. All my thoughts were centred on what might lie ahead of me.

My arrival at the penitentiary caused a stir as no Jewish prisoner had been admitted there for well over a year. The goal of the Germans, after making Germany Judenfrei, free of Jews, was now to empty all prisons of their Jewish inmates. No doubt to make room for the many offenders, political and non-political, who were overcrowding the prisons to bursting point. The difference between a prison and a penitentiary in Germany was not really noticeable at first, except that the inmates in the latter were there on a much more permanent basis. Most of them were common criminals with very long sentences. Many had been behind bars for more than twenty years. But there were others. At the time of my arrival there were, I think, some five women awaiting execution. They had been sentenced to death for having committed treason, sabotage or some other crime against 'Greater Germany', such as distributing anti-Nazi tracts, spreading defeatist rumours or sheltering a wanted person.

When I was shown my cell, I was pleasantly surprised. The cells in the penitentiary were much larger than those in the prison and, being the only Jewish inmate, I was spared sharing a cell with other women. I was considered a dangerous influence on others, having been sentenced for helping the enemies of the Reich and for forging papers in order to escape from Germany! It was a blessed relief to be by myself, although I missed my sister dreadfully. Very soon I got acquainted with the daily routine, which differed a little from that of a prison. The regime was a lot harsher and the working hours longer; but the food was better and the time allotted for the daily walk in the courtyard was substantially longer. But there was one great drawback: in prison we had walked together with the other inmates; in the penitentiary I had to walk by myself: round and round in the same prescribed circle, my hands behind my back, and forbidden to look up lest I should catch a glimpse of some face at one of the innumerable small, barred windows. Our guards behaved no better and no worse than the ones in prison – with one exception. There was a small woman with jet-black hair which she wore in a tight bun. She came from Siebenbürgen, a part of Romania that had been settled by German immigrants during the last century. That woman, whose German was no more than rudimentary, and who had inherited the virulent anti-semitism that has always been a feature of certain sections of the population in Romania, concentrated her venom on me. She never missed a chance of taunting me with my imminent demise in a gas chamber. She hit me when I inadvertently committed some offence against the rules and regulations, and generally made my life miserable. But there were compensations.

Although officially I was not allowed, and had no opportunity, to talk to any of the other inmates, I occasionally got little messages of encouragement whispered through the crack in my cell door. The longterm inmates, whose job it was to clean the halls and corridors of the penitentiary, and who also distributed food at meal times, had observed me on my solitary walks and had taken a liking to me. They thought of me, I suppose, as a kind of pet. I was by far the youngest girl in the building, and I profited from their small acts of compassion. At meal times an extra potato would be pushed through the half-open cell door, and often during periods when the guards were not walking around, these women came to my door and talked to me. They were all of them common criminals, guilty of murder and other crimes. None of the political prisoners were allowed to work outside their cells. But these Kalfaktors, as they were called, the hardened criminals, few of whom would ever be free again, were the only inmates who ever gave me any word of comfort or compassion during the time I was in Jauer Penitentiary. As I was kept in solitary confinement, I was not permitted to go to work with the other prisoners. Instead, work was brought to me in my cell. Even after so many years, I shudder when I think of my first task, in which I failed disgracefully. I was supposed to knit grey woollen socks for the soldiers. But wool at that time was already difficult to find, so I was given smelly, stiff grey socks which I was told to unravel; I was then to tie the small bits of wool together and proceed to produce knitted socks. When the lady in charge of allocating work came back the next day, I cried and confessed that I just could not do what she had asked of me. She took pity on me, and from that day onwards until the end of my stay in Jauer I became an accomplished maker of shopping-nets in all the colours of the rainbow. I have no idea how many nets I produced in the six months I was there, but I remember that I was once warned by one of the Kalfaktors that I should reduce my 'zeal' because the other prisoners resented being told that the Jew-girl in

No.9 made twice as many nets as they did. The explanation for my devotion to work was simple: it helped pass the time. In the end I decided to continue at my working speed but to unravel the nets that exceeded the accepted daily quota. We were allowed one book a week and as I was always a quick and avid reader, I tried to ration myself and keep the book for Sundays, when we did not work. Although I soon got caught up in the daily routine, I did not fool myself into thinking that I would be able to spend the three and a half years of my sentence in Jauer. Even in solitary confinement in a cell in one of the best guarded penitentiaries in Germany rumours penetrated to me. One day, when I had bad toothache and was taken to the dentist, I managed to exchange some words with another prisoner. She had for some mysterious reason been transferred from Auschwitz to Jauer. It was from her that I learned for the first time what till then I had refused to believe: that every single horrible thing that had been whispered about Auschwitz was *true*.

A few days later I was called to the office of the Chief Warden, and as I was clattering down the iron stairs in my wooden clogs, I knew that my days in Jauer were numbered. Standing next to the Warden was a man in a leather coat who handed me a document and ordered me to sign it. It was the official order for my transfer to Auschwitz.

Renate Lasker

5

'Voluntary' Transfer to Auschwitz

There were some 5000 concentration camps set up by the Nazis. However, when one thinks about these camps, usually the names of only a few of them like Auschwitz, Bergen-Belsen, Buchenwald and Dachau spring to mind. I don't believe that there was much to choose between them. Their main distinction was their size and the methods by which the inmates were murdered. The camps were mostly set up in the vicinity of ammunition factories so that the inmates could be used as cheap labour. Auschwitz and Belsen probably made the biggest headlines after the war. Belsen was liberated by the British Army and what was found there at the liberation defied description.

Auschwitz got its reputation because it was the biggest concentration camp of all, and its method of killing people and subsequently disposing of the bodies was probably the most sophisticated in the annals of genocide.

Auschwitz, or Oświęcim as it was called before the Germans invaded this part of Poland, was established in 1940 because the Germans felt that it was imperative for a concentration camp to be built there. They anticipated mass arrests in the area. The first transport of Poles was sent to the camp in June 1940. Millions of people were sent to Auschwitz from all the countries the Germans occupied, and it became more and more overcrowded. An extension camp was established about two miles away from the original one. The name of this was Birkenau. The building of Birkenau began in October 1941 with prisoners from the main camp being sent there to do the work.

I myself did not arrive in Auschwitz-Birkenau until late 1943, and therefore did not personally witness the appalling circumstances under which the new camp was built. The conditions have been described well enough by people who were there at the time.

To come back to my own part in the story, the trial was over, and Renate and I returned to our cell with a sense of relief at being back in familiar surroundings, and perhaps the tiniest ray of hope that we would remain there together just a bit longer. It was too much to hope for. As Renate says herself, two days after our return to the prison cell she was called down, and we knew that the moment of parting had come. We had had so many partings before – parents, friends – but this was different: although we tried to be optimistic in the face of the overwhelming odds against us, I don't think that deep down we had too many illusions. As time marched on, it was bringing us closer to our own fate. The only thing that was not clear in our minds was what form that fate would take. Being together was such a tremendous comfort. We could talk about the 'old days', and sometimes manage to see the funny side of things in the monstrously over-filled cell in which we were confined. I became an accomplished imper-sonator of some of our guards; we sang canons together; and we did sometimes laugh. Without any doubt, we propped each other up. That was to come to an end now, and a new situation had to be faced. This time we both had to face it alone. As Renate recounted, the actual parting was not too long drawn-out since everything in prison always has to be 'quick, quick, quick' (just as in concentration camps). It seemed more than improbable that we would ever see each other again.

So Renate went off and I remained in the cell adjusting to this new turn of events. It was at that point that Miss Neubert, who supplied us with the material for our work, started chatting to me more extensively. She wanted to know in particular where my sister was. I looked forward to her visits. In fact they became the focal point of my long day. She became a real friend.

Although I was in this impenetrable fortress and not allowed to talk to anyone, I have mentioned that much did filter through. I somehow got to know that it was unlikely I would remain in the relative security of my prison cell for the duration of my sentence. The prisons were getting more and more congested, and a simple way to make space for new arrivals was to empty them of their few remaining Jews, as Renate pointed out, and send them off to concentration camps. By this time there were all sorts of rumours about conditions in the camps, and especially about Auschwitz and the gas chambers, and I too now had to come to terms with the bitter truth that this was precisely what was ahead of me.

It would be dishonest for me to say that I was not scared, but in an odd way one can get so accustomed to being scared that it becomes part of one's make-up. We had lived with fear – in a general sense – for so many years that it had become merely part of the background. But now that I was confronted with the real thing, I knew it was only a matter of time before I was called down. I was actually more frightened of losing a limb or becoming crippled than I was of death itself. I clearly remember some agonizing nights when I did not sleep at all because of the dire prospects. Like Renate, I had become well informed about the goings on in Auschwitz. Prisoners sent back to my prison from Auschwitz for further interrogation had also confirmed the rumours about the gas chambers. There was less and less doubt in my mind about what the future held for me. However, human nature is mysterious. In the face of all this evidence – and probably because the thought of being put to death like vermin was too much to bear – I somehow managed to set myself 'outside' what was actually happening. There was a Bible in our cell and I became an avid reader of it. I learned whole chunks of it by heart. I know that this helped a great deal. I could keep my 'enemy' at arm's length and I almost hypnotized myself into a state where I felt untouchable. I could never accept that one human being could have the right to destroy another. Call it what you will – fatalism or faith – I convinced myself that nobody could touch me unless a higher power decided otherwise. It was my way of coping at the ripe old age of sixteen. I was certainly not unafraid, but I may have appeared to be fearless. The other thing was that I despised my persecutors with such a depth of feeling that I think that it emanated from me in some way. I was rarely the target of physical abuse.

The day came and my name was called. It was early December 1943. I had to go for a 'medical examination' – can you believe it? – and sign a piece of paper to say that I was going to Auschwitz 'voluntarily'. The medical examination was even more grotesque than the 'voluntary' bit. Since I was past caring about any possible consequences, I asked the Gestapo doctor why the hell he was bothering with a medical examination when he knew as well I did where I was going. He did not reply. It made me feel better at least to have said *something*. I was taken back to my cell, and a few days after that I was called down again. I seem to remember that Thursday was Auschwitz day. I was given my civilian clothes – it was a good job that there was something left of them – and put in a cell of my own to await transportation.

Miss Neubert's visit, very much at her own risk because she had absolutely no business being in my cell since I was no longer painting toy-soldiers, and the food, greetings and little proverbs she passed on to me from her mother were an enormous morale-booster. If ever there was anybody in need of a morale-booster, it was me. I have spoken about this earlier, but

I think it can bear repetition. It was one of the very rare good experiences I had in that period.

I left the prison the next morning. First I was put in a 'black Maria', and then I boarded a train with proper cells into which I was locked together with a number of other prisoners, and off we went in an easterly direction. We arrived in Auschwitz–Birkenau in the evening. I don't know what time it was, but it was dark. We were taken to a barracks, and there we had to wait. When I try to recall my first impressions of Auschwitz, what comes to mind is black figures in capes, dogs barking and a great deal of shouting. We, my travelling companions and I, waited in that barracks until daybreak. I was not aware at the time that I had already overcome the first hurdle. As a rule, when transports arrived at Birkenau, there was a reception committee of SS men who made a 'selection' there and then of who was to enter the camp, and who was to go straight to the gas chambers. I did not have to go through this selection process, and I only came to understand the reason why later on: I had not arrived in one of the standard, huge transports, but I had been sent with a prison transport of relatively few people, all of whom had been the subject of court cases and had been given prison sentences. That classified us as Karteihäftlinge, that is, prisoners with a file. This status meant that we could not be sent straight to the gas chamber, allegedly so that we could be available in case we received a summons to reappear in court. Though useful on arrival, it made no difference whatsoever to our treatment once we were inside the camp. Clearly, it was better then to arrive in Auschwitz as a convicted criminal than as an innocent citizen.

At the first light of day, we were taken to a different barracks or 'block', as I shall call it from now on. There the 'welcoming ceremony' took place: I had to take my clothes off, my head was shaved and the number 69388 was tattooed onto my left forearm. It was done, as I only slowly realized, not by Germans but by prisoners whose job it was to work in that block.

I find it impossible to come to a firm conclusion as to which of the 'initiations' was the most traumatic.

The tattooing was not a pleasant experience, especially if you bear in mind how primitive the tool with which it was carried out was. It looked something like a penholder except that instead of a nib it had a thick needle at the end. Of course it hurt. There was blood and a nasty swelling afterwards. Very likely it became infected. I don't believe for one moment that this tattooing tool was ever disinfected. I suppose I should regard myself as fortunate in that the girl who tattooed me had reasonably neat handwriting. The numbers that now adorn my left forearm are not outsize and all over the place like some I have seen. Maybe the shaving off of my hair was in fact the most traumatic experience. It made me feel totally naked, utterly vulnerable and reduced to a complete *nobody*. By now I had relinquished my clothes as well, and I stood there stark naked, without any hair and with a number on my arm. In the space of a few minutes I had been stripped of every vestige of human dignity and become indistinguishable from everyone around me.

While this initiation was going on, the prisoners performing these tasks kept bombarding me with questions. Everybody was starved of news from the outside world. The girl who processed me asked where I came from, what my name was, how long I thought the war would last, and what I was doing before I was arrested. I told her all I knew, which was not much since I had not been a 'free' person for a considerable time before arriving in Birkenau. She also asked me whether I would give her my shoes as they were going to be taken away from me anyway. I naturally agreed, and I took them off and gave them to her. I will never know what prompted me to tell her that I played the cello. It might have seemed a superfluous piece of information under the circumstances, but I did tell her, and her reaction was quite unexpected. 'That is fantastic,' she said, and grabbed me. 'Stand aside. You will be saved. You must just wait here.' I did not know what on earth she was talking about, but I did what I was told. I stood aside clutching a toothbrush, which I did not realize at the time was itself a great privilege.

I stood and waited, for what I did not know. By that point the block was deserted and horrifyingly resembled what I had come to expect a gas chamber to look like: there were showers overhead ... I did not know that I was actually in the 'sauna', or bath-cum-delousing block of the camp. I was sure that the very moment had come for which I had tried to prepare myself through those long anguished nights in prison. Yet again, everything turned out differently from what I could have reasonably expected. In those early days I had but the vaguest idea how the gas chambers functioned. I was to learn a lot more about them later. All that happened was that a handsome lady in a camel-hair coat wearing a headscarf walked into the block. I had no idea who it could be. Was she a guard or was she a prisoner? She was so well dressed that I was absolutely baffled. She greeted me and introduced herself as Alma Rosé. She was simply delighted that I was a cellist, and asked me where I came from, who I had studied with, and so on. The whole thing was like a dream.

The last thing I had imagined when going to Auschwitz was that I would ever have a conversation about playing the cello. Remember, I was still naked and holding my toothbrush. Alma was very happy to hear of my arrival, and again I heard the words: 'you will be saved'. She said I would have to go into the Quarantine Block, but told me not to worry: somebody would come for me soon and I would have an 'audition'.

The Quarantine Block was the first, and for many people the last, port of call in the camp. Conditions there were abominable. The sleeping quarters consisted of a type of shelf – or Kojen, as they were called – on which everyone lay like sardines. Most of one's time was spent on 'roll call', in German the term was Appell or Zählappell. This meant that one stood outside the block five deep in the freezing cold, inadequately dressed, in order to be counted. I never understood the German mania for counting people. Since they were so preoccupied with destroying as many of us as possible, why was it so important to account for everybody? However, there it was, and enduring Appell was a sort of torture itself. You were strictly forbidden to move, and because the procedure lasted an eternity, it will be clear what that meant for the prisoners who, almost without exception, suffered from dysentery. In plain language, many of us just stood there with shit running down our legs, in complete agony. How easy it was to call us 'dirty smelling pigs'. It is impossible to convey how extreme our misery was.

Very fortunately, I did not remain in the Quarantine Block for long. One day an SS officer came and called for 'the cellist'. His name was Hoessler. He took me to the Music Block, and there I saw Alma Rosé again – and a whole lot of other people with instruments.

6

Music for the Inferno

So this was the Lager Orchester, the camp orchestra. And for me it was clearly audition time. Alma gave me a cello, and asked me to play something. I would like to remind whoever may read this that I had not seen, let alone touched, a cello for nearly two years at the moment I am describing. I asked Alma if I could have a few minutes to 'reacquaint' myself with a cello, and I had a little practice. I seem to remember that I played – or tried to play – the slow movement of the Boccherini Concerto. When I had finished, I sat down and joined the camp orchestra. There was no real danger of my not passing the audition; for up to the moment of my arrival the orchestra had not had a single bass instrument. There were a number of violins, mandolins, guitars and flutes and two accordions (one of which was played by a Dutch girl called Flora and the other by a Greek girl called Lilly Assayal, who, as I found out years later, became Murray Perahia's first piano teacher). My audition piece with the orchestra was the *Marche Militaire* by Schubert, and it was also easy enough to be well within my grasp. Anyway, Alma was overjoyed at the addition of a bass line.

Thus started both my career as the only cellist in the camp orchestra, and my life in this small community, which was to generate the warmest friendships and camaraderie as well as hatred in equal measure. I shall try to describe the motley crowd that made up the orchestra.

I left the Quarantine Block the day after my audition and moved into the Music Block. It is all so long ago now that only essential things come back to me, or the things that must have been significant at the time. I shall never forget my first evening there when I met the prisoners with whom I was to live in such close proximity until we were finally liberated. But that day was far off, and none of us really believed it would ever come.

The people I remember most vividly are Hélène, or 'la petite' Hélène, as she was called, who was French, and 'la grande' Hélène, who was Belgian and was the leader of the orchestra; and Violette, who played the violin, and Elsa, both of them French. Once more I was thankful to be able to speak French because this at once made me acceptable to the French-speaking contingent as well as to the German-speaking one, among whom Hilde became a good friend.

We sat in a circle and I was 'interviewed'. There were the usual questions: what news did I have of the war; what was I doing before the war, etc? Much to my surprise 'la petite' Hélène lit a cigarette and handed it to me. My first cigarette for months and months. It was blissful. I puffed away, and talked and talked. Much later, when I had made friends with her, she told me that she had nearly passed out when I took one puff after another and just held the cigarette in my hand without handing it on to the next person. She had not wanted to say anything at the time because I was the 'new girl'. But I soon learned that cigarettes were a very expensive commodity, and changed my smoking style. We 'organized' cigarettes by paying for them with bread. Bread was extremely precious (a gross understatement), and it was not surprising that Hélène was less than happy with my first smoking 'performance'.

In an absurd and irrational way, I had the feeling that there was more freedom in the camp than I had had for ages. Suddenly there were people to talk to, and I was no longer locked up in a small cell all day. I had been sitting on my behind for many months, my routine interrupted only by the half-hour circular walk in total silence. But this relative 'freedom' was an illusion. Here in the concentration camp you were really and truly trapped and the only way out was via the chimneys.

I was once asked on TV – and I was quite unprepared for the question: 'Weren't you scared out of your wits all the time you were at Auschwitz?' Interestingly, my answer was 'no'. I have often thought about it since, and the only explanation I have is that fear is like an ache. If you live with it long enough, you do get used to it.

As I sit here writing, I am more and more conscious of my inability to convey fully what Auschwitz-Birkenau was like. Essentially it was a programmed death-factory. Many other books have been written about Auschwitz, and if you wish to find out more about it, it should not be too difficult. I feel that the best contribution I can make here is to talk about *my* life there.

My experiences were of course different from those of the vast majority of prisoners for the simple reason that I was lucky enough to be in the orchestra. The obvious advantages apart, I think that probably the most

important thing was that, although my head was shaved and I had a number on my arm, I had not lost my identity totally. I may no longer have had a name, but I was identifiable. I could be referred to. I was 'the cellist'. I had not melted away into the grey mass of nameless, indistinguishable people. I never gave the matter any thought when I was there, but today I am convinced that in a subtle way it helped me to maintain a shred of human dignity.

However, the background was the same for all of us. The smoking chimneys were a constant reminder that this was an extermination camp as well as a concentration camp. One might be engaged in some sort of work, as in the nearby factories, but it was only a temporary existence and, short of a miracle, there was no particular reason to suppose that one would get out alive. All the same, as long as there was life, there was hope. 'Hope' is not in fact a good word to use because theoretically there was no way out whatever. And yet one kept on battling for survival by sheer instinct. Which brings me back to the orchestra, and in particular to Alma Rosé, who was the supreme example of this instinct for survival.

One of the unusual features of the Music Block was that Jews and Aryans lived in it together. The only prerequisite for being there was that you had some more or less remote idea how to hold or play an instrument. Any excuse was good enough to attempt to rescue as many people as possible and bring them into this relative haven. Some people who could not really play at all were taken in. Their task was to copy music because all the works we played had to be arranged and re-orchestrated for our peculiar collection of instruments. They were the Notenschreiberinnen, the music copyists.

Our main function was to go to the Main Gate every morning and every evening and play marches for the thousands of prisoners who worked outside the camp, at places like I.G. Farben, inter alia. It was imperative that these columns of prisoners should march neatly and in step, and we provided the music to achieve this. We sat out there in all weathers, sometimes in subzero temperatures, scantily dressed, and we played. In this uniquely strategic position we witnessed all sorts of things. For instance, prisoners unlucky enough to be caught with 'treasures' which they had managed to 'organize', hoping that they would not be frisked by the SS, would be made to kneel down and eat whatever they were caught with. I once saw a woman being forced to eat a packet of cigarettes.

A typical day in our commando, as it was called, would proceed as follows. We would get up one hour before dawn. Some of us would have the duty to carry the music stands and stools 'nach Vorne', which meant to the gate of the camp. When this had been done and everyone was back in the block, we would have to stand for roll call. For us, in our privileged position, it was held inside during the winter. We would stand in rows of five and wait to be counted.

After this we had a hot drink, which was not easily identifiable as anything in particular, but it was hot, and we ate whatever we had managed to save from the previous evening. Then we marched out, again in ranks of five, to the Main Gate. We sat down and started to play our marches for the outgoing commandos. These were accompanied by Kapos, SS and dogs. When that was over, we would return to the block, and the people who had taken the stands and stools out went back to fetch them. Finally, we started to rehearse.

Alma Rosé was the leader of the Lagerkapelle in the fullest sense of the word. She certainly was a most remarkable woman. She was the daughter of Arnold Rosé, the famous violinist, who had been leader of the Vienna Philharmonic Orchestra for many years, and also had a well-known quartet. Her mother was the sister of Gustav Mahler. She therefore had a unique musical background. Alma was herself a very fine violinist, but her most notable quality was her powerful personality. She commanded absolute respect from us, and to all appearances, from the SS as well. Her position was unprecedented. Alma had started her life in Auschwitz at the infamous 'experimental block', Block No. 10, where Prof Dr Carl Clauberg, a gynaecologist, made experiments in sterilization. It was discovered that she was a musician of some standing, and she was subsequently 'rescued' and put into the position she occupied when I met her.

If anybody has ever been faced with a challenge, it was Alma – in an unheard of situation, and confronted with a most unusual collection of instruments that were played by an equally unusual collection of 'musicians'. One could have counted on the fingers of one hand the people whom one could really have called 'musicians'. Among the most accomplished were Fania Fénelon (not to be confused with Fanny) and Lilly Assayal. With this material Alma set herself the task of creating a genuine orchestra, in which only the highest standards were acceptable. They were the standards she herself had grown up to respect. In reality it meant that Alma had to drill practically everybody note by note, and she threw herself into the task with a fervour that seemed ridiculous in the circumstances. We must not forget that outside our little world the gas chambers were working non-stop.

Alma was relentlessly strict, and gave us severe punishments for playing wrong notes. I remember that I had to wash the floor of the entire block for a whole week on my knees for playing badly. I had just returned from the Revier (the sick bay), where I had miraculously recovered from typhus. It was the type of typhus that was rampant in the camp. Commonly known as 'Flecktyphus', it was transmitted by lice. If you had been fortunate enough to recover from it, or escape the 'selection' which was made regularly in the Revier, it left you unbelievably weak, and usually with impaired eyesight and hearing for a while. I myself returned to the Music Block in such a deplorable state and had duly been punished by Alma for my inadequacies.

I should add at this point that when I was lying in the Revier, I was mainly unconscious, although I have a vague memory of seeing some SS men at the end of my bunk, and of hearing someone say, 'this is the cellist', and moving on … The normal procedure for the selections at the Revier was that everybody was herded out of their bunks and made to stand naked in front of whoever was conducting the selection; and you either 'passed' or, more likely, did not 'pass'. I certainly would not have passed, for I could barely stand on my feet.

I was back in the Music Block, then, not playing very well, and washing the floor as a punishment. I could not say that I loved Alma for this. In fact I was furious and hated her. But strange though this may sound, I now have nothing less than the greatest admiration for Alma's attitude. I am still not sure whether she took a premeditated line or acted on instinct. But with this iron discipline she managed to focus our attention away from what was happening outside the block, away from the smoking chimneys and the profound misery of life in the camp, to an F which should have been an F# …

Perhaps this was her way of trying to keep sane, and by involving us all in her frenzied pursuit of perfection in our performances of the rubbish we played she may well have been instrumental in helping us to keep sane ourselves. There is no doubt that we owe Alma the greatest debt of gratitude. She would not tolerate anything second-rate, and the highest praise she would give if we played something well was: 'this would have been good enough to be heard by my father … ' She frequently talked about her father, and repeatedly said to us that, should any of us survive, we should try and find him and tell him about the orchestra. I was glad that I was able to fulfil her wish. I saw Arnold Rosé when I came to London and we talked about Alma. He died shortly afterwards. She obviously did not rate her own chances of survival too highly in spite of her relatively privileged position. Her disciplinarian attitude towards us was never prompted by fear of the SS, or of any dire repercussions if we did not play as well as we should have done. She was a proud lady, aloof and very dignified, regardless of whether she was dealing with us or the SS, and I am certain that she was deeply respected, even by the SS.

In addition to our twice-daily outings to the camp gate, we had other functions as well. We 'gave concerts', believe it or not, most Sundays, sometimes in the open air, between the A and B camps, or in the Revier. Also we always had to be ready to play for any SS personnel who came into our block for light relief after their exhausting work of determining who should live and who should die. It was on such an occasion that I played Schumann's *Träumerei* for Dr Mengele.

Our repertoire consisted of pieces such as German hits of the period, various selections, *Czardas* by Monti, *Zigeunerweisen, 12 Minutes with Peter Kreuder, Blue Danube, Tales from the Vienna Woods,* arias from *Rigoletto, Carmen,* and *Madame Butterfly,* Dvořakiana, the *Marche Militaire, Träumerei,* and so on. I cannot recall everything we played, but you can see that it was a real miscellany. The music was supplied by the SS in the form of piano reductions which then had to be orchestrated and written out.

I must now tell you about the quite extraordinary coincidence through which I was reunited with Renate.

Just to remind you, Renate and I were separated in prison in Breslau when she was taken out of our cell and sent to the penitentiary in Jauer. We did not expect to see each other again.

The key objects in this tale were a pair of shoes made of pigskin. My mother had bought them for me when we were still a 'family'. I was proud of those shoes. One day, I spilled something on them and they were ruined. The only way we could save them was to dye them black. She was extremely cross with me. Anyway, the shoes looked a bit dismal now that they were black, and so I got some red laces with bobbles to cheer them up. Even more important, it made them eminently recognizable. As I have told you, on arrival in Birkenau we had our heads shaved, we were tattooed, and we had to give up our clothes; and on that occasion I gave my shoes to one of the girls who was chatting to me while the process went on. She clearly wanted the shoes for herself, and since I was going to lose them anyhow, I saw no reason not to give them to her. Little did I know what effect this transaction would have. I had been in

Block for only a week or two when this same girl came running into the block and asked me to come immediately to the Reception Block with her. She said, 'I think your sister is here … ' I raced over, and there she was. It was incredible. You need to take into account the vast size of the camp to appreciate the enormity of the coincidence. What had happened was that my sister had arrived with a transport from Jauer and was being processed by the very person who had processed me shortly before. Renate noticed her shoes and asked where they came from. When she heard that they had belonged to someone who came through a short while ago and was now in the orchestra, she knew instantaneously that this could only be me. That was how we found each other again in the endless chaos. It was truly a miracle. Poor Renate had had a ghastly time, but I was able to help her to a certain extent. You have already read her account of life in Jauer. It was not a bed of roses, but compared to life in Auschwitz-Birkenau it must have appeared cushy.

Being together transformed things for us. It gave us an added incentive to survive, for each other. Renate deteriorated very rapidly in Auschwitz. She did not have the good fortune I had had, and she had to go – and stay – in the Quarantine Block.

I have spoken about conditions there. They were beyond description. Renate became a total wreck in no time at all. It was horrifying. Her appearance and general state were so bad that she was not allowed to enter our block. So she came and stood outside, and waited for me to bring her some soup, or whatever else I could give her. She developed huge festering sores on her legs which would not heal. They were caused by Avitaminose, a total lack of vitamins. Eventually she contracted typhus and all seemed lost. There were times when I hoped that she might quietly die so that her misery would be brought to an end. It was awful watching her sinking. I don't know how, but she survived the typhus and she emerged from the Revier looking even more frightful than when she went in. It was then that I made a desperate move. I thought I had nothing to lose, and I went to see the camp commander, Frau Mandel. I told her that my sister was in the camp and asked whether it would be possible for her to become a Läuferin, a messenger. This was a very good position to have in the camp. It meant that you stood at the entrance gate ready to run errands for whoever needed to send a message to some block or other. But above all it meant better rations and marginally better housing. There were two things in my favour when I approached Mandel. One was that I spoke German and the other was that Mandel was a champion of the orchestra. I was pretty sure that she would not have me 'put away' (for want of a better word) for my audacity, since I was irreplaceable as the only cellist in the camp.

I thought that the worst that could happen was that she would ignore my request. Improbable though it may seem, she was quite polite, and she said she would see what she could do. She merely wished to know which block my sister was in. And indeed, shortly after this 'interview', Renate became a Läuferin. Naturally I was worried that Mandel would change her mind the moment she clapped her eyes on Renate, whose appearance was anything but prepossessing. However, she didn't and for Renate that was the difference between life and death.

In time she regained some of her strength and obtained better clothes. The advantage of the job was that it got you to all parts of the camp and gave you endless possibilities for 'organizing'. Organizing was camp parlance for bartering. I can safely say that the cello saved not only my life but my sister's life as well.

Somehow we kept going. It is strange that, as I sit here trying to recall things that I have been trying to forget for so many years, one particular feature of Auschwitz springs to mind. It is the nasty yellow mud which appeared as soon as the weather became bad. I suppose the ground was clay, and the mud covered one's footwear. It was 'verboten' to have dirty shoes, and one fought an endless battle to wash them. The more I think about it, the more I realize that, for me at least, it is not possible to describe life in Auschwitz-Birkenau adequately. Certain words and images do come to me, though, and will convey some of the ingredients of this hell on earth ... the stench of burning corpses ... smoke ... hunger ... despair ... screaming ... 'Muselmänner' (emaciated people, in camp language) ... And yet behind all the hopelessness a kind of life somehow still went on.

There was another side to Auschwitz which is rarely talked about, perhaps because it is more marginal and must appear even more incomprehensible than the horror the name Auschwitz stands for. Enormous wealth accumulated in these few square miles. When someone knocks on your door and you are told to get ready to leave home, usually in a great hurry, and take what you can carry, you choose whatever is most practical: warm clothes, jewellery (if you happen to have any left), and the things that are precious to you and might be of some value one day, God knows when. The result during the war was that thousands, no, millions of people converged on a relatively small patch of earth carrying their most treasured worldly possessions. Some of them were musical instruments, and that, I believe, is how I came by a cello in Auschwitz. As I have explained, everyone was stripped of their possessions on arrival, and these were all gathered together in a huge warehouse, known in camp language as 'Canada', probably because Canada was considered to be a wealthy place. To work in 'Canada' was the height of prestige because it was the source of all things valuable and useful. 'Canada' was a paradise for 'organizing'. The camp currency was bread, and there was nothing whatever that could not be obtained from 'Canada' – and that is where my red jumper came from. When I acquired it, it was a nice warm jumper and it cost me a lot of bread. Incidentally, it was made of angora wool, which for some unknown reason was also 'verboten'. However, I got hold of it and I wore it incessantly right up to the liberation, always well concealed of course. I still have that tattered and torn jumper today among my 'souvenirs'. Its condition speaks volumes. (It is now an exhibit in the Imperial War Museum.)

Auschwitz was also a microcosm. With connections and bread you could obtain anything. There were some people who were very 'wealthy'. Every block, for instance, had a Blockälteste (or Blockova), that is, a block-elder. They could boss you around at will, and they were the people who arranged for the collection of bread for the block from the kitchen and distributed it. The loaves were cut into four portions, and what could have been easier than to make those portions a bit undersize and keep the rest for your own purposes? That was where the camp currency came from. The camp had a highly developed hierarchy and was run almost entirely by it. To be a Kapo or a block-elder meant that you belonged to the aristocracy. The abuse of power by some of these people was legendary. There were notable exceptions. One was a Belgian girl called Mala, whom everyone admired. She was the chief interpreter in the camp and had great integrity. She was caught trying to escape from Auschwitz with her Polish boyfriend, and we were forced to line up and watch her execution. She made a heroic last stand, producing a razorblade she had managed to conceal and cutting her wrists while shouting abuse at her executioners.

The Blockova of our block was a certain Czajkowska, a Polish woman. She had been in charge of the orchestra before Alma's arrival – and that was before my time too. Then we had a Stubenälteste, a sort of 'head girl'. Her name was Pani Funia. I can see her now. She must have had facial paralysis because her mouth was all to one side. She doled out the soup; 'Po Zupe, Dziewczynki', she used to shout. Her face and voice are etched into my memory.

Harmony did not always reign in our block. We were too much of a mixed bag for that. Our nationalities and the languages we spoke were very diverse, and there were Jews and non-Jews together in the same block, as I have mentioned. There was bound to be friction. Some of the Poles, for instance (the non-Jewish ones), occasionally received parcels. They were a group apart and there was no earthly reason why they should be expected to share their parcels with anyone else. Receiving a parcel did not only mean added nourishment. For us Jews, being deprived of them underlined the fact that we were totally isolated from the outside world and abandoned to our inevitable fate via the chimneys. But our isolation did create a feeling of being together 'in the same shit'; and firm friendships were formed between some of us. It is very important not to underestimate the mutual support we gave one another. I think we all contributed a little to each other's survival. We watched everyone and bullied people when, for example, we noticed the first signs of slacking in personal hygiene. I shall never forget the time I was ill with jaundice. I am no longer sure whether it was in Auschwitz or Belsen. I could not endure the eternal turnip soup any longer and my friends, as a matter of course, fished whatever bits of potato they could find out of their soup, collected them together, and gave them to me. It is hard to take in now what this meant to me. Giving up a piece of potato was a great sacrifice. We have most of us kept in touch over all the years that have passed since the war, and that must speak for itself.

Some years ago, I met my great friend Hilde, who was copyist to the orchestra, for the first time since 1945, and it felt as though we had never been apart. I maintain a close friendship with 'la grande' Hélène who lives in Brussels, as I did with Fanny who also lived there until she died – both of whom helped us so much later on in the story – and with Violette, whom I probably see more frequently than any of the others. I am glad that I am in contact again with two of the Polish members of the orchestra, Helena and Zofia. We met in Krakow in September 1994. Still somewhat hampered by language difficulties, we managed to talk to each other in spite of it, and in place of mutual distrust we have established a good and honest relationship. Some of us have died since the liberation, and I think of all those people with great affection. What I really want to say is that, contrary to the way in which we were portrayed in Arthur Miller's film version of the camp orchestra, we were far from being a vindictive mob of unruly girls who stole from and betrayed each other at every opportunity. In spite of many differences in character and background, we were a very positive small community of people, sharing a miserable life and the prospect of a miserable end. What was positive was the concern we had for each other, our warmth and friendship. I would like to quote from a piece Fanny wrote some years ago:

[translation from the French]

... I have a wonderful memory of the marvellous understanding that reigned among us. Particularly the brave little gestures by which we gave each other the courage to hold out; the hope we gave each other when there was no longer anything to hope for; and the bread we shared. We remained human beings, and for those who lived through the life of the camp, it is a great achievement to have been able to preserve their dignity. I am proud to have been part of the orchestra. In my opinion we were all responsible for each other's conduct ...

Fanny Birkenwald

It is a pity that Fania created such a misleading impression about the camp orchestra when she wrote her memoirs which were subsequently made into the film. For reasons best known to herself, she indulged in the most preposterous distortions of the truth about practically everyone who took part in this 'drama'.

Actually, when these events took place, Fania was a valuable member of our community. No one can recall anything with which to reproach her. Hélène, for example, fondly remembers how she used to tell her fairy tales in order to take her mind off grim reality. Hélène had been very young, sixteen or perhaps seventeen, and Fania was a good deal older than most of us. She was one of the few accomplished musicians there, and I shall never forget the evening when we played chamber music in Auschwitz. Fania had a remarkable musical memory and transcribed the *Pathétique* sonata by Beethoven for string quartet, and we played it one evening. It may not sound very extraordinary; it was just a chamber music evening. But it was one with a difference. We were able to raise ourselves high above the inferno of Auschwitz into spheres where we could not be touched by the degradation of concentration camp existence. I have been reminded by one of my friends that that evening was the occasion for some anti-semitic outbursts. I can't say that I remember this. Very probably I chose to forget it.

Alma died on 4th April 1944 in Block No.4. There were many rumours about her death. There was talk in particular of her having been poisoned by the Kapo of the 'Canada' Commando, Frau Schmidt, whom Alma had visited the night before she fell ill. She was taken to the Revier, where she died a few days later. I do remember Alma complaining of blinding headaches and the general consensus was that she died of meningitis. We were all extremely upset and felt very insecure.

I have recently been shown an excerpt from part of a book written by a friend of Alma's who was with her when she died. But even this is not conclusive about the cause of her death, although alcohol poisoning is mentioned (see Appendix 3 on page 153). That Alma was given special treatment was borne out by the fact that we were all called to the Revier, where we filed past her body which was laid out on a white cloth. Even the SS seemed upset.

The word 'insecure' may seem another odd one to use but with Alma no longer there it soon became clear that she had *been* the orchestra. She had held it all together. Alma, with her strong and dignified personality, had liaised with 'the other side', that is, the camp commanders like Mandel and Drechsel, to get supplementary rations for us, among other things. But most important of all, with Alma's demise we were deprived of leadership in a much wider sense. We continued our daily outings to the Main Gate to play our marches, but when we returned to the block to rehearse old and new repertoire, we felt her absence acutely. One of our 'colleagues' was a Russian girl by the name of Sonya. She was a singer and a pianist – quite good-looking – and of very mediocre talent. She was a favourite with the SS and she was nominated as Alma's successor. It was a total disaster. Nobody respected her and the whole orchestra became a free-for-all.

Shortly after this crisis the Hungarian transports began to arrive. It was now May or June 1944. Thousands upon thousands of Hungarians poured into the camp. The death machinery was totally unable to cope with the influx – gassing, murdering, burning. The crematoria worked round the clock. In the end, people were thrown into the flames alive. In the course of one day the SS managed to murder 24,000 people.

With these transports, several musicians arrived who joined our ranks. I can't now tell you all their names, but Eva Steiner, a singer, who survived, was one of them and above all there was Lilly Mathé. Lilly was a violinist who had travelled all over the world with a gypsy boys' band, and was very well known. She was a warm and generous person and her contribution to the orchestra was considerable. We started to play a lot of Hungarian music such as *Czardas* by Monti, and she helped to keep the SS interested in the orchestra for a bit longer. But Alma was irreplaceable.

We hardly had any news of events outside the camp and we had no conception of how the war was progressing. We existed from day to day, always apprehensive about how long the status quo could continue.

And then, one day – I think it was the end of October 1944 – the next moment of crisis came. We were ordered to 'line up': *Jews* to one side, *Aryans* to the other! It could only mean one thing: the *gas chamber*.

… I recall that I was terribly anxious to contact Renate, so that she should know what was going on. It soon transpired that we were not going to be gassed but instead were going to be sent to another camp.

7

From Hell to Hell:
Our Miraculous Escape to Belsen

It is bizarre that we all thought this was some kind of a miracle. Nobody could believe that we were actually going to leave Auschwitz by the Main Gate. We were blissfully unaware of what was still in store for us.

The first thing that happened was that we had to take our clothes off and we were given a new outfit. By that point most of us had managed to 'organize' relatively acceptable clothes. Now we had to give these up and we were issued with real monstrosities. It brought it home to us that our 'cushy' time was at an end. I did, however, manage to keep my famous red jumper. Somehow, Renate must have heard about this latest development for the orchestra and she appeared on the scene. Once again we were faced with the prospect of separation. The thought of being separated now was unbearable for both of us, and it was the most natural thing in the world for her simply to join us. Nobody stopped her. We boarded the familiar cattle-truck, and departed. We had no idea where we were going. I know now, though did not know then, that the Russian front was approaching fast from the east, and that our evacuation was part of a plan to leave as little evidence as possible behind for the Russians to find. Why that particular day they bothered to drag us right across Europe when they could so easily have fed us into the gas chamber, I shall never comprehend.

We started our journey westwards. There were rumours flying about – there was never any shortage of them – that we were heading for a 'convalescent camp', an Erholungslager, and that it was called Bergen-Belsen. Nobody had ever heard of it.

It is only today, after reading a book about Belsen, that I am able to understand how it got the reputation of being a convalescent camp. I will give you a brief history of this infamous place. When I was actually on the way to it in the cattle-truck, I was not too interested in the origins of Belsen. All we knew was that we were *moving*, and that was all we needed to know. We were moving *away* from Auschwitz, away from the gas chambers, and we were happy, if I can use such a word.

The first barracks in Belsen was built as early as 1935-6. It served as accommodation for workers who had been brought in after the local peasants had been resettled elsewhere. The idea had been to build an 'exercise complex' for the German army where it could hold manoeuvres. When the work was complete, the barracks was supposed to be used as a storage place for weapons. After the capitulation of France in 1940, it became a prisoner-of-war camp for French and Belgian prisoners, who were made to enlarge it. No sooner had they started on their work than the Germans and Russians changed from being allies to being bitter enemies. In 1941, huge transports of exhausted Russian prisoners arrived in Belsen and had to camp in the open air as there were no barracks ready for them. Some 14,000 Russians came altogether. In spite of constant new arrivals the overall number of prisoners in the camp never increased very much because of high mortality. Dreadful epidemics raged and an average of 300 prisoners died every day. By 1942, it was practically empty. The surviving Russians were sent to do agricultural work in nearby villages. Early in 1943 Belsen was made into a Lazarett or military hospital camp for prisoners of all nationalities, and I expect it was this which gave rise to the idea that Belsen was a convalescent camp. Only a part of the existing camp was used for these purposes. The remaining section accommodated 'privileged Jews'. These were Jews of foreign nationality who were kept apart as possible exchanges. They included not only foreign nationals but people who had some sort of entry permit to various countries. They never reached their destination, but perhaps they deluded themselves into thinking that they might get away somehow. By the middle of 1943 Belsen had acquired yet another title. It became an Aufenthaltslager, a residential camp. Presumably that distinguished it from a Vernichtungslager, or extermination camp.

But we knew nothing about all this as we moved westwards. The journey took four days and we were very, very cold. We tried to warm ourselves up by blowing with all our might against each other's back, with our mouths placed directly onto the person concerned; and we cheered ourselves up by singing our orchestral repertoire, each of us taking her own part. Whether we had instruments or not, it seemed clear that we were going to remain together. One day the train stopped, not at a proper station, but apparently in the middle of nowhere. There followed the usual 'reception': SS guards ... screams ... 'schnell ... schnell ... schnell ... raus' (quick, quick, quick, out). We fell out of the train, lined up five abreast as usual, and started marching. That I remember little about our trip in the cattle-truck is again symptomatic of the necessity for some experiences to be pushed out of one's mind.

The Lüneburger Heide, or Heath, is well away from human habitation. We marched along for a considerable distance and never saw a single civilian. We were merely aware of the sound of continuous shooting. This was not very encouraging, to say the least. What is more, I spotted a signpost which read: 'Zu dem Schiesstand'. In gothic script the Z and the J look similar, and I promptly read it as 'Juden Schiesstand'. Schiesstand means rifle range. I was convinced that this was where we were all going to be shot. It did seem rather absurd that we had been conveyed all this way in cattle-trucks only to be shot on arrival. But there never was much logic in the Germans and their murder-machine. Anything was possible. I only hoped that I would be shot first. I did not want to see Renate and my friends being shot, and I thought that was what would happen because I was in the first row. We continued marching in silence, past the rifle range. The noise never stopped. But nobody shot us. Finally we arrived at the camp, Belsen Camp. What we saw was not promising. A few barracks blocks, some big tents and some water-pipe lines raised above the ground. Renate reminded me the other day that we noticed somebody with a Kapo armband bending over a soup vat and scraping it out. She had remarked drily: if a *Kapo* needs to do this, things must be bad. I am afraid she was right. Things were bad. Very bad. But not nearly as bad as they were to become.

The biggest problem at the beginning of our stay in Belsen was that there was no room for us. I believe our part of the camp held about 1000 people, and we were 3000 new arrivals. These figures may not be absolutely accurate, but the fact remained that there were *no quarters for us*. It was winter. We stood in line, and we were issued with one blanket and eating utensils. Then the circus began.

We were taken to our new 'home', and found ourselves confronted with several huge tents. There was nothing inside them, and what it is like in reality herding hundreds of people into a tent is impossible to put across. Common sense told us that it was essential to create gangways so that people would be able to leave the tent when they had to relieve themselves. It may sound simple enough, but I assure you that it was not. Everybody just piled in. All one wanted was just to lie down somewhere. Anywhere. For some reason, my friend Hilde and I took it upon ourselves to attempt to organize some sort of a system. No doubt it was our Germanic upbringing. It was a thankless task. But without gangways everybody would be trampled on by whoever had to leave the tent, and life would become even more unbearable than it was anyway. I recall that we screamed and shouted, and tried our best to get people to lie down in rows. Whether we had any success, I don't know. But at least we tried. For some days we lived like this. In a great big heap, on the bare ground in a flapping tent, cold and wretched. But if we thought that these were scarcely the most desirable conditions, and that we had reached rock bottom, we were very much mistaken.

There was worse to come. One night a terrible storm broke out over Lüneburg Heath, the rain pelting down. It proved too much for the tents. They collapsed on top of us in the middle of the night, and that was that. It was pitch dark and there we were, with the tent flattened, and everybody struggling to get free. Somehow we managed to untangle ourselves. When we finally achieved this, we just stood there in the open in the pouring rain, the wind howling, for the rest of the night. It is astonishing how much the human body can endure. We were all deeply undernourished and badly clothed – in short, not in the pink of condition. And although it was freezing and we were drenched through, I did not even catch a cold. That would have been out of the question in normal life. One would have caught not just a cold but pneumonia. It will for ever remain a mystery to me how we survived that night without serious after-effects.

When morning came, we were taken to a warehouse stacked full of shoes. What joy … We had a roof over our heads. We were of course told that if anybody as much as touched a shoe, they would pay dearly for it. I am not sure how long our respite in the shoe-bunker lasted. I do remember that it became very boring, and that I sat next to a Hungarian woman and thought that this might be a good opportunity to learn a little Hungarian. How mad can you get? I am afraid I was not very successful. Hungarian is hopelessly difficult. But it helped pass the time. We were pretty cramped in our shoe-bunker because the place was after all full of shoes and not meant for human habitation. But at least we had shelter. Before long, our stay in the bunker came to an end. Suddenly and inexplicably there were barracks available for us to move into. It was said that these barracks had been occupied by Russian prisoners and that they had been murdered: there had been a Russian PoW camp there and thousands of Russians had perished. Now, after reading the history of the camp, I believe there was some substance to the rumour. The only thing I cannot say with certainty is that the Russians were killed in order to make room for us.

The name Belsen conjures up pictures of heaps and heaps of unburied corpses and human skeletons moving about among the corpses. My courage has begun to desert me as I try to tell you what it was actually like living in this place. I am fully aware that Belsen is in every way indescribable. All the same, I shall attempt to tell you something about it.

Although we were no longer an 'orchestra', we continued to function as a group. It happened quite naturally and without any discussion, and was undoubtedly one reason for our continued survival. We watched each other like hawks for any signs of giving up. It was tempting not to strip and wash every day in the freezing cold of the winter. The water supply was outside. We saw ourselves getting thinner and thinner, and shared whatever food we could get hold of. In those early days, Belsen looked different from the pictures we have seen of it in films. There were no mountains of corpses littering the camp. There was nothing to do. We merely existed from one day to the next. A thing I remember clearly was that news got around that someone had died in the block. There it was, a dead body: the first of so many. It was obvious that this body had to be moved and put outside. I cannot say who came with me, but I stood up and took on the job. I had never touched a dead body before, and I did not really want to do it, but something made me. I probably wanted to prove to myself that *nothing* was impossible. A form of conceit, I suppose, but in an unexpected way it gave me strength. Fairly soon corpses became so commonplace that one ceased to take any notice of them.

Belsen was not equipped to cope with anything - least of all with the sick and the dead. It did not possess the 'facilities' available in Auschwitz, where bodies could be 'processed' with comparative ease. Auschwitz was a place where people were *murdered*. In Belsen they *perished*. As brave Germany shrank in size before the advance of the Allied troops, more and more people arrived in Belsen. Camps all over Germany were being emptied and attempts made to erase any trace of them. Thousands and thousands of prisoners were on the march.

The death marches are recorded on film, but the experience of seeing these poor people arriving literally on their knees was devastating. Needless to say, the prisoners who managed to reach the camp more dead than alive were the 'lucky' ones. Thousands fell by the wayside.

Our own situation had now changed. We had been put to work. We were sent to a makeshift factory called a Weberei, and the work consisted of weaving together cellophane strips – we could only guess what this

might be for. The finished article was some kind of ersatz rope. It was not
an inspiring occupation, but it was one all the same. Typhus was raging
everywhere and it caught up with those of us who had not had it in
Auschwitz. If you have typhus and happen to survive it, as Renate and I
had, it makes you immune. One heart-rendingly sad case I knew of was
that of Ibi from Hungary, who died of the disease after the liberation.

The days went by, and the weather improved. Although it was a relief
not to be freezing all the time, conditions in the camp continued to deteri-
orate. Food became sparser every day, and then we began to have days
without any food at all. People died like flies. Corpses began to pile up
and decompose in the warmer weather. We moved about like zombies.

At this point, Renate was working in the office of the 'administration'
and was able to bring back encouraging news about the progress of the
war from time to time. It was evident that things were not going well for
the Germans, but that knowledge was somehow not enough to keep us
'cheerful'. We knew – I don't know how – that camps had been blown
up before they could be liberated. It was not surprising. Who wants to
be caught with millions of rotting corpses on display? So in a way, we
scarcely dared to hope. But it was hard to come to terms with the fact
that we still might have to die before the nightmare came to an end.

Conditions became even worse. Feeble attempts were made to clear
away the corpses. We were ordered to drag them along the 'Lager Strasse',
but to no great avail. There were too many corpses and we were too
weak. (Renate describes the same operation on page 95.) The whole scene
was like hell. Eventually there was no food at all, and I have a vivid memory
of seeing somebody kneeling (as a punishment) with a human ear in his
mouth. It was the beginning of cannibalism. Strangely enough, it only
occurred among the men. But I don't believe it was widespread. Every
day that one woke up and remained alive seemed a miracle.

I am aware of my inability to give an account of everything I experienced. There is much that I have 'swept under the carpet'. I think that is
definitely necessary if one wants to survive and retain one's sanity.

I have been asked: 'How is it possible that so and so managed to survive
this or that camp?' To me it has implied that 'survival' was somewhat
suspect and must have been achieved by foul means such as collaboration
with the Germans, or that survival was due to some special physical or
mental strength. Such questions sadden me greatly. The short answer is
that the odds were a hundred to one against your being alive at the end
of the war if you were an inmate of Belsen, or any other concentration

camp for that matter – and there were hundreds of them. If you did witness the day of the liberation ... you were simply lucky. You were a 'survivor'.

But I am jumping ahead. We were not liberated yet. The name Irma Grese may ring a bell. She had been a guard in Birkenau, and one day she appeared in Belsen. She was always accompanied by a dog. There was much publicity in the papers about her when she eventually sat in the dock at the trial in Lüneburg in 1945. She was good-looking, or so the British press thought, and therefore deserved more attention than the other ugly brutes. In reality, she was as mean and vicious as the rest of them. Anyway, Irma Grese came up to me one day in Belsen and started to make 'friendly' conversation. It was unheard of. I can't recount the exact conversation we had but I do recall that she used the word 'we' (me and her) as though we belonged to the same species. There could be only one explanation for her sudden friendliness: she was trying to create a space for herself in my heart by being so pally. It was obvious: the end must be near. Grese was sentenced to death in Lüneburg, and hanged.

More and more transports kept arriving and people – if one could still call them people – kept pouring into the camp in their thousands. Now we had to endure the lack of food and water for days on end. I must mention here that it was discovered after the liberation that our misery could have been alleviated to some extent at least. There is documentation in Eberhard Kolb's book *Bergen-Belsen* to show that some 500 woollen blankets had been delivered to Belsen. Also 1700 tins of Ovaltine were found and a huge amount of food, tins of meat, biscuits, and so on: enough to fill a room 12 x 15 feet in area and 10 feet high from floor to ceiling. It had all been sent by the Red Cross, and none of it was ever distributed. Large quantities of medicaments were found as well. These supplies were later used by the British troops to help us.

All we knew at the time was that, one way or another, the end was really at hand. It was excruciatingly clear that without food or water we could not live much longer. In addition, we were certain that the Germans did not want to leave any traces of their misdeeds behind. It had become a race. Would the Allies reach us in time?

8

The Liberation of Belsen

Other unusual things were happening. We saw less and less of the SS personnel. Indeed, we hardly saw anybody at all. We had been abandoned, and although we should have been elated by the thought that freedom was in sight, we were not. I remember that I was actually angry most of the time. We had been holding out for so long, and had suffered so much, only to be blown up at the finish ... It must have been the withdrawal of the SS that made us so suspicious and convinced us that this was their plan.

When somebody suggested to me that the constant rumbling noise we could hear in the distance together with the intermittent shooting might – just might – be British tanks approaching, I was absolutely furious. I simply could not allow myself false hopes that might be dashed at any moment.

When I heard the first announcement through a loud-hailer and saw the first British tank, I flatly refused to believe my eyes.

At this point I will include an account Renate wrote of the day of the liberation:

[translated extract from a script she wrote for television]

April 1945 was exceptionally hot. I remember this well. It is sometimes difficult and sometimes easy, too easy, to remember things one would rather forget or suppress. But I can feel the oppressive heat now and smell the unbearably sweet smell of naked decomposing bodies, especially when I shut my eyes. Now half a century has gone by, and a new generation has grown up, a generation which is probably as bored of hearing about concentration camps as we were with the stories of the front line in the Great War that my father used to tell us. But I was going to talk about 15th April 1945, the day of the liberation.

Many of the events of the day are rather hazy but I remember certain details. In the morning I left my sister in the care of a comrade and went in search of water. Anita lay on a bunk, very sick, and was murmuring incomprehensible words. She had a high temperature. It could not be typhus because we had already had that in Auschwitz. But she was not in a good state. We had not had any bread for several days. The soup that was occasionally distributed in minute quantities was mainly water, and quite undrinkable. I had managed to 'organize' a rusty bucket and went to the camp entrance. There was an apparently harmless SS man standing guard, and he did not attempt to stop me. I was making for the one and only water tap that was still functioning. It was near the administration barracks and that was deserted.

The Germans had evaporated. No one at all stopped me. I filled my bucket and returned through the gate. There I was met by a horde of prisoners, half dead with thirst, trying to get hold of some of the water ... The bucket was snatched from my hands, the precious liquid spilled into the dust and disappeared. It was a hopeless undertaking. I returned to my barracks empty-handed. I helped my sister off her bunk and led her out into the open air. We sat on the ground, leaning against the hut. In front of us ... next to us ... corpses.

A few days earlier the SS had tried to get a commando to move the bodies to a big ditch. We had been given some string to tie the arms of the dead together and then drag them along the main thoroughfare in the camp. But we did not have the strength. The 'operation' was discontinued and the bodies remained where they were.

Then it must have been mid-day. For days we had heard the rumbling noises of heavy artillery, but we hadn't known who was firing. We had had no idea what was happening to us. The noise came closer ... and then ... a voice through a loud-hailer ... first in English and then in German. At the beginning we were too confused and excited to take anything in. But the announcements kept being repeated, again and again. At last we understood: BRITISH TROOPS ARE STANDING BY THE CAMP GATES ... PLEASE KEEP CALM ... YOU ARE LIBERATED ... We were also told – and this was not news to us – that there was typhus in the camp, and that we should wait for the troops to come. We should be patient ... medical help was on its way. It took a while for the significance of these announcements to sink in.

When the first tank finally rolled into the camp, we looked at our liberators in silence. We were deeply suspicious. We simply could not believe that we had not been blown up before the Allies could get to us.

R.L.

The date was 15th April 1945, as Renate has said. A date no one will ever forget. It was a Sunday and the time of our liberation was approximately 5 o'clock.

I would like to be able to describe how it felt to be liberated. That would be a daunting task even for a professional writer. For years we had been subjected to the extremes of emotion and hardship. Despair – fear – hunger – misery – hatred – friendship. There is only so much one can take. We were completely burnt out.

Our experiences in the war had been well beyond the scope of what would normally be piled on people during the course of a lifetime. And suddenly, it was over. We were 'liberated'. Another monumental experience. After years of living for the moment and perhaps, if we were lucky, for the next day, all at once there was space in front of us. It was very hard to believe. I was nineteen years old and felt like ninety.

I doubt whether anything could ever match the feeling of relief, incredulity and gratitude which began to seep into our consciousness as we slowly dared to acknowledge that it really was true ... We were alive, and the soldiers who were walking about in the camp were not our enemies.

You must realize that we and our liberators saw the camp with different eyes. We had lived surrounded by filth and death for so long that we scarcely noticed it. The mountains of corpses in their varying degrees of decay were part of the landscape and we had even got used to the dreadful stench. It would be wrong to assume that everything was instantly transformed the moment the first tank entered Belsen. What the British Army found was far removed from anything it had ever had to deal with, even in wartime.

In my collection of memorabilia I have a number of reports written by army personnel. I must have picked them up in the office where I worked as an interpreter (which is actually a bit of a joke since I did not speak English then). Some excerpts from these will give you an idea of what Belsen looked like from the British point of view:

... On 12 Apr 45 following the break-through of the Second Army after the Rhine crossing, the German Military Commander at Bergen-Belsen approached 8 Corps with a view of negotiating a *truce* and avoiding battle in the area of BB Concentration Camp.

1. My father, Alfons Lasker, 1884-c.1942 (deported)

2. My mother, Edith Lasker (née Hamburger), 1894-c.1942 (deported)

3. My grandmother, Flora Lasker (Grossfloh), who died c.1942 (deported)

4. My father (*left*)

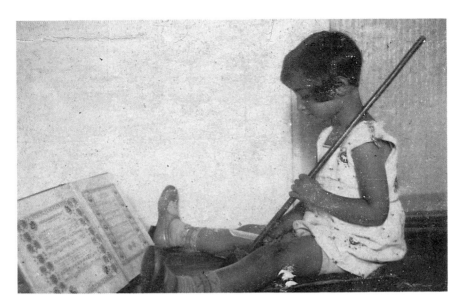

5. Myself, aged about three, pretending to play the cello with a broom and comb

6. Marianne, myself and Renate (*left to right*) in about 1930, Breslau

7. Renate, myself, Marianne and my mother *(left to right)* in about 1931

8. Weinhold Schule, the primary school where I had my first anti-semitic experiences
(*myself top row, third from left*)

9. Myself, aged 12–13, in 1938 in Berlin, where I studied the cello with Leo Rostal

10. My uncle, Edward Lasker, 1885-1983

11. My father (*left*) and uncle Edward, his brother

12. Myself in 1939

13. Renate in 1939

14. Marianne making furniture in my father's defunct office, Breslau, 1939

15. The family in 1939, still intact and living in the apartment in Kaiser Wilhelm Strasse (later renamed Strasse der SA) *(left to right: myself, Renate, Marianne, my mother, my father)*

16. A room in our apartment in Kaiser Wilhelm Strasse, 1939

15

16

17. Kaiser Wilhelm Strasse 69, Breslau, where we lived, with a statue of Moltke in the foreground

18. Breslau law court and prison today

19. Alma Rosé with her Wiener Walzermädeln in the late 1930s

20. Auschwitz, 1944: the arrival of a transport from Hungary
(reproduced by courtesy of the Wiener Library)

21. Auschwitz, 1944: Hungarians queuing up to go into the gas chamber
(reproduced by courtesy of the Wiener Library)

22. Belsen, about 19th April 1945: SS personnel carrying bodies to the mass graves,
guarded by British troops
(British Official Photograph No.BU 3799 (XP), Crown Copyright)

23. Belsen, 1945, mass grave no.3

24. Belsen, 1945, deserted camp

25. Belsen, interpreters' house in Displaced Persons' camp about two miles from the main camp

26. Myself on the boat from Ostend to England, 18th March 1946

27. Myself in 1996 (*photograph by David Jacobs*)

In occupation of the area were 800 Wehrmacht, 1,500 Hungarian soldiers with their families and certain SS prison guards.

In the Concentration Camp were known to be 45-55,000 internees of whom a large number were reported to be suffering from typhus, typhoid, tuberculosis and gastroenteritis.

The electricity and water supply had failed and there was no bread and very little food ... In the interest of our troops and the internees and from the point of view of preventing the spread of disease a *truce* was granted on the following terms:

The German Military Authorities were to erect notices and white flags at all road entrances marked: *Danger Typhus* ... German troops and Hungarian troops would remain at their posts wearing white armbands on their left sleeves ... The Hungarians would remain indefinitely and were placed at the disposal of the British for such duties as may be required. The Wehrmacht were to be released within six days and conveyed back to the German lines with their arms and vehicles. The SS personnel were to remain at their posts and carry on with their duties ... etc etc.

This truce sounds pretty naïve with hindsight, but when it was negotiated, there were still three days to go before the first tank entered the camp and nobody could possibly have envisaged what they were going to find there.

Here is another quotation from a report, *Notes on Belsen*, which was written at a much later date:

... The first British Tank Unit to arrive at BB was Anti-Tank Battery of 63 Anti-Tank Regiment ... The scene which met the First Comers beggars description. There were appr. 50,000 people in the camp of which about 10,000 lay dead in the huts or about the camp. Those still alive had no food or water for about seven days, after a long period of semi-starvation. Typhus, among other diseases, was raging ... filth everywhere ... the air was poisoned ...

This might give some idea, however remote, of what it was like.

Of course we, on the other side of the fence, were unaware of the difficulties the British Army was facing. To have to cope with thousands of dead and half-dead people was certainly not part of army training. Many, many mistakes were made in those first days. It was obvious that it was imperative to prevent us from leaving the camp. Soon after the repeated announcements told us that we were liberated, that we should keep calm, and that help was on the way, the tanks left the camp. The reason was that they had indeed had to go and get help, but it created a most unfortunate situation.

It would be pointless to lay blame on anyone in particular for what happened next because it was the result of confusion, helplessness and ignorance. We were left in the camp guarded by the Hungarians who manned the watch-towers – the very same Hungarians who had been fighting alongside the Germans. They were an extremely trigger-happy bunch and shot into the camp at random. It was all pretty chaotic. I dare say they were scared out of their wits about what would happen if we got our hands on them.

I am not sure how long this pandemonium lasted. Soon more and more British soldiers returned to the camp. They all looked like gods to us. They were totally shattered by what they saw, and in their desire to help us as much as possible, they produced lots of food. That proved to be another serious mistake. Nobody was used to eating, certainly not tins of meat, and many people died after this sudden intake of food. I don't remember how Renate and I avoided the danger, but we did, and gradually we began to appreciate our new circumstances.

We were free and no longer had to fear for our lives.

I cannot be certain of the subsequent order of events, as I cast my mind back to those early days after the liberation. I see it roughly in two phases. The first lasted up to the moment when the flamethrowers arrived to burn the camp down on 21st May 1945. The top priority had been to clear the camp of corpses. This time the work was done by the SS guards who had not managed to get away. *We* had become the spectators, and the British soldiers were hard pushed to keep us in order and stop private lynching parties from forming.

By God, it did not take long for those former SS guards to look abjectly dishevelled. I wonder what went through their minds as they cleaned up their handiwork. They loaded thousands of corpses onto lorries and then stood on top of them as they threw them down into the mass graves. It was Dante's Inferno!

This mass burial is amply documented in the film *A Painful Reminder*, which permits me to dispense with any attempt to describe it.

We were not fully in the picture about everything that went on behind the scenes. It must have been a mammoth task to rehabilitate the survivors, find hospital accommodation, doctors and medicine and generally try to get some order into the chaos. One immediate task was to discover the identity of the people who were still alive, and make a register of their names and nationalities.

The British looked around desperately for people who could speak English, and Renate, who had studied it when she was at a boarding school in Florence before the war, had occasion to use her knowledge for the first time. She became an official interpreter almost at once.

As we began to believe that we were not dreaming, that we really were alive, and that we had a future before us, we discussed how we should go about letting our family – what was left of it – know that we still existed. But how do you do that in the middle of a war? The answer came sooner than we had thought possible, in the shape of a van. Someone rushed up to me and told me that a BBC van was going around the camp, and that one could record messages if one had anyone left to send a message to. So off I went and met Patrick Gordon Walker who was manning it. (He was to become a Member of Parliament, or perhaps already was one by this time.) He was very kind and understanding. It was no easy task for me to be confronted with a microphone and talk. I have a transcript of my 'talk' in my files. It is a translation because I could not speak any English then. It seems a bit garbled, but it did the trick.

My message was broadcast repeatedly by the BBC and it was eventually heard by a neighbour of my sister Marianne's, who was still living in England. She immediately got in touch with Marianne, who in turn heard the message herself when it was re-broadcast a few hours later. I have often asked myself how Marianne must have felt when she heard my voice. She had never dared hope for one moment that we had survived, and there was no postal service yet, as the war was not over. The first return message from her came by courtesy of the British Army. In time we were able to establish a system by which our letters were posted by soldiers whose addresses and numbers we used for the replies.

On 21st May the last part of the barracks was burnt down by flame-throwers. The swastika and a picture of Hitler had been attached to it and there was a ceremony. We all stood there watching as this final vestige of the camp was devoured by the flames. We were transferred to what had been a German military establishment, some two miles away from the original camp. By now we had formed ourselves into a little group of 'interpreters', and we were given quarters in a small wooden house which had probably been the gardener's lodge when it was in German hands. It was a nice house (see plate 25), and most certainly preferable to the impersonal stone buildings in which all the other survivors were billeted.

9

Peace at Belsen:
Secondment to the British Army

Contact with Marianne
Our life as interpreters was quite congenial. Being attached to the British Army meant that we had all sorts of privileges. In my scrapbook I have umpteen 'passes' to testify to them. In particular, we were allowed to use the officers' bath at certain times, and to move freely in and out of the camp. That may sound odd, since we were in effect free people; but in reality the conditions under which we lived were still far from normal.

I wrote my first letter to Marianne after we had moved to the new camp:

Belsen Camp, 25th May 1945

Dearest old Marianne,

I am sitting in the office without much to do; so, abandoning my plan to wait for news from you, I will write you a few words ... We are now living in a small cottage. It is first-class. We have two rooms upstairs, a radio and very nice furniture. We eat in the army canteen. The food is much too good. Renate has had to start watching her figure. In brief, we are rejoicing in our new life. I really mean that.

I am waiting very impatiently for news from you, and for photographs of the family. Mrs Horwell has written saying that I spoke on the radio but that unfortunately you did not hear the broadcast, and that some friends told you about it. I believe it has already been repeated three times. Maybe you will pick it up sometime. Please don't forget: every time you see Mrs Horwell you must give her our inexpressible thanks for all her help. Quick, quick, do write us a letter!!!!!!!!!!!!!!!!!!!!

Greetings to everyone who would like to have greetings from us: especially your husband whom I shall get to know with God's help *soon* ...

We kiss you ten thousand times,

A and R

Belsen Camp, 26th May 1945

My beloved Marianne,

It is hard – very hard – to cope with being unhappy and miserable, but happiness is even harder to cope with. We had your first handwritten letter of 15th May today via Mr E Johnston. I keep reading it over and over again, and cannot describe to you how happy we are. 'Happiness' is not a strong enough word. I could easily shout out quite mad things to anyone passing by.

You ask what we are most in need of … Marianne, we are longing for one thing. *Please* send us some photographs: of you and your husband – and if it's possible of our parents and of home. Also a dictionary would be very useful. Nothing apart from that. We have masses to eat and plenty of cigarettes: we get army rations. And the question of clothes, which is no worry to us as we are used to wearing what we stand up in, will be dealt with here. All this is under control. For us there is only one thing: our dear old Marianne is alive and well …

I must thank your friends with all my heart just for being your friends and ours, and for trying to achieve the unachievable, something that for us is unimaginable. You know what I am talking about. We have learned to be *patient*.

I am counting on having a letter from you within the next few days. I am tired and I am going to bed now. It is cosy here. Radio, warmth, light and a clean bed. Inconceivably precious things.

Good night … greetings to all,

and for you all my love

A

Belsen Camp, 2nd June 1945

Dearest Marianne,

The bearer of this letter is going on leave tomorrow and I am taking advantage of it to send you a direct message. Here are thousands and thousands more kisses. I will write down the address which you should now use:

13070559 Cpl Smith AG, HQ 35 Group Pioneer Corps, BLA

but also please try using the following address *once only*: Anita Lasker, Interpreter attached to No.1 War Crimes Investigation Team, Belsen Camp. Just as an experiment … Do write *soon*. We can scarcely bear it.

When we receive your first letter addressed direct to us I will be able to write very differently. And please, please send us some photographs ... With the wonderful weather we are having at the moment, it is even more difficult to believe that we are really *alive* ...

All our love, Yours A

Belsen Camp, 4th June 1945

My beloved Marianne,

Still no direct news from you. So far we have only had your letter via Cpl Johnson in your own handwriting. I don't want to be unreasonable, but I know you must have had our pictures by now and have written back straightaway, and I am sad and worried that I have not heard from you. Lt H's address can't now be used because he has suddenly gone on leave, and I presume you have used that. God knows where the letters can be flying about. I am alone at home, it is 8 p.m. and the Bruch Violin Concerto is being played on the radio. The weather is splendid and I think life is beautiful. Perhaps, perhaps, perhaps, if the heavens are favourably disposed towards me I may in the not too distant future become the owner of a C-E-L-L-O. I can hardly wait. Tomorrow will be a sad day for us. By now you will be familiar with Hélène, the plump little French girl, from the photographs. I was with her in the concentration camp throughout this period, and we are very good friends. When people have spent years together, as we have, and have shared every crust of bread and every cigarette, it becomes a very special kind of friendship. She is going back to Paris tomorrow morning by plane, where she is hoping to find her sister ... She will leave a big gap behind her when she goes ...

I will be shortly sending you a good article about Belsen Camp. At the moment I am busy making some copies – or rather Renate is – since a lot of people would like one. Write very soon!!! and about everything ...

Greetings to our friends and to the family ... Write!!!

Thousand kisses and love, Yours A

PS ... You will soon get a visit from a certain Lady Montgomery. I need not explain anything particular about her ... Please have complete confidence in her and go over all your plans for us with her. She has a big say here, and may be able to help us. Apart from that she is a most charming lady.

Once more, a thousand kisses, Yours A

Belsen Camp, 6th June 1945

Beloved M,

I am very happy that you will be receiving some firsthand news about us from the messenger who delivers this letter to you. I am nervous writing it. He will tell you about certain things one cannot very easily write about. He will be returning here after his leave, and I hope he will bring me fresh news from you. Maybe you will even be able to give him some photographs. They will reach me with absolute certainty. Every day we start by hoping that we will have some post from you, and at the end there has been none. We are very, very sad. Renate is translating the *Fire Regulations for the Camp* into German, but she will interrupt her work for a moment and write to you. She is cross that *I* am always writing.

I hope that we will at last be hearing from you. Please [this part is written in English] 'excuse that I write such a stupid letter without any sense, but I am so nervous this morning, that I am not able to write another letter. You must understand that it is quite difficult for us to write something reasonable, because there are plenty of new things coming in our mind, and if even we have a quiet hour, we must take all our strength together to be quiet ourself. I am afraid you may not understand my "English" but I hope later on I'll be able to write properly in English … '

I kiss you a thousand times with all my love.

With God's help we will soon (?) *be together again?*

Yours … all yours, Tita

This is a family letter.

Belsen Camp, 8th June 1945

My dearest loved ones,

It was almost too much today: within half an hour I had two letters. One from that funny Rabbi, the one with the photographs. I had barely left his office to go to mine when I found the second letter: the one that came via Cpl Smith; and yesterday we had the one via Sgt CC Warner. Renate hasn't yet heard about the latest two letters because she has been away for the day on a car trip acting as interpreter. It is impossible for me to keep all this happiness to myself. Luckily there have been many good friends about to share my joy and look with interest at the photos. But who can really grasp what it means to me to see you all like this, so happy, and – even if this is not the right way to put it – so unsullied by the bottomless filth of the past three years? ... How can I describe what I feel when I see you again in these photographs ... I have been so moved by your concern for us. You know, when I read your letters I went hot and cold ... I must just ask you one thing: please *don't* send us any clothes. We don't need them. We get everything we need. We are about to be fitted out from head to toe. One of the officers here has made this useful occupation his personal hobby, and he doesn't have any real problems with it since he is 'in charge of the stores'. We have been given some stockings, and this week we will be having skirts and short jackets made for us. We have also got some blouses. I personally prefer walking about in navy-blue trousers, and think that the less one possesses the happier one feels ... I have only one request - and it may sound funny when linked to the name Belsen: in the next few days a *swimming pool* will be opened in the camp, and we would like to get hold of some swimming costumes, and perhaps you could find some flat-heeled sandals? We both wear size 39 shoes. But please, only if it isn't too much trouble. Otherwise there's nothing we need. We are waiting impatiently for the dictionaries ... And if it's possible Marianne, could you send some music? To give you an idea of what I need: Joseph Merk's *Studies for Violoncello*, Bach's Cello Suites, Sevčik's *Bowing Exercises* ... These would be the most urgent items. Even more *urgent* would be a cello of course, but since I have raised merry hell with all the high-ups here, it might even materialize at the same time as the music does. I feel I am being terribly demanding and unreasonable. It is midnight and horrible insects are buzzing around my lamp. Renate is squawking that I should put the light out. I am tired and I will do as I am told. Good night my dearest.

Continuation tomorrow morning ...

Saturday, 9 a.m.

... Two things to ask you, and please reply: how come Harry knew of our existence a few months ago? I find this totally baffling.

... Our greatest wish is that we should all meet again in England. Yes, it is *truly my greatest wish*, however we manage to get there, whether it is via Switzerland or direct. I do so much wish to see you, Marianne, while you are still in England. This does not mean that I have relinquished the idea of Palestine ... I have learned that it is useless to battle against fate ... Belsen Camp is Belsen Camp, and however free of worries our life may be at the moment, it is just a passing phase ... If only you knew how much I would like this 'phase' to lead to England eventually. Marianne, I hope you understand: I have not abandoned Palestine!!!!! Only please, please let the springboard for our new life be England ... You mentioned that we still have some money owing to us from our parents. I don't at the moment know what money it is you are talking about – only that Count Künigl has all our suitcases, the grand piano and all the furniture and carpets in storage in Hungary, and also that he has far-reaching obligations to our father, or rather to us ... He behaved impeccably right up to the last moment. When our parents were arrested, he immediately came to Breslau and did everything he could to prevent their deportation. That he was unsuccessful was due to Mr Fey. The name should sound familiar [he was Gestapo Chief in Breslau].

But even if he had been able to prevent it, we would have been sent to Auschwitz with the last Jews in March the following year, and we would not now be in the happy position of being able to correspond with one another ...

I have recently been in Hanover, and also in Hamburg. It gives me no pleasure to see such total devastation, however much I hate the Germans – and yes, I do *hate* them without exception, if you can grasp what hating means. It goes so deep that if I have to speak to them (and for me in my capacity as 'interpreter' this happens frequently), *I have to turn away from them to stop myself hitting them in the face: every single one of them, even if they have not done anything to me personally*, and say that they have no knowledge of the horrors of the concentration camps ...

Talking about Hamburg: the devastation of the towns in Germany – it is a fact, I am an eyewitness. There is hardly a house left standing. It is another link in the chain of destruction, above all the destruction of precious values, without rhyme or reason. On 8th May, one minute after midnight, the continuation of this destruction was forbidden and it was called *peace*. When I drove through Hamburg, I felt ashamed, not for myself, nor for Germany – I feel nothing for Germany – but for the human race. I felt ashamed for the whole human race. I hope you understand what I am saying ...

Renate wrote this letter:

Hanover, 9th June 1945

My beloved Marianne,
   ... When I returned last night after a tiring drive, Anita had a surprise

for me. Four letters from England ... and to cap it all: the photographs!!!
... When I look at the ones of our parents I find it impossible to believe
that we really will never see them again. Oh, Marianne, it is sometimes
very, very difficult ... Do you really think that we will be able to join you
soon? ... I should tell you that during the past three years I have used up
all my energy. The reaction is just setting in now. I only have one wish:
that there should be peace and harmony, and that we can hope that life
will have something good in store for us. The question of whether we
would want to go to Palestine is a difficult one to settle, especially as we
have learned not to plan too far ahead. At the moment, all we think about
is having a reunion with you in England. The most important thing is
that we should stay together. You can feel happy wherever you have
friends and good people around you ... It seems incredible that you can
be untainted by the filth and horror we have experienced ... How beautifully you have written about our beloved parents!
   ... Ten thousand loving kisses

Reh

Searching for a new life

It may seem strange, but I began to grow bored. My closest friends, Hélène
Wiernik, Hélène Rounder and Violette Silberstein, and all the others who
had countries to go back to, had left Belsen and gone 'home'. No one
had had any idea what they would find on their return but at least they
had somewhere to start searching. That was not the case with us. It would
not have crossed our minds to consider Germany or Breslau, by then in
Russian hands, as our 'home'.

For the record I must mention something here that I have only found
out quite recently: it is that Jewish army personnel had a fight on their
hands to convince the officers in charge of 'repatriation' that they should
not divide the survivors into their respective nationalities and then help
them to 'return home'. The complexities for our liberators in sorting out
the unprecedented chaos were enormous; but it could not be expected
of the average British army officer who had been sent off to fight a war
that he should be able to grasp fully the significance of the term 'displaced
person'. That was precisely what we were, displaced persons. The question
was, where could we be 'placed'?

For the moment we were still in Belsen, and very slowly exchanging
our preoccupation with death for a new concern: *life*.

```
BELSEN CONCENTRATION CAMP                          PASS 'B'
                                           SERIAL No ...118...

No .......... Rank ...........    Name ANITA LASKER...
INTERPRETER ATTACHED TO CMP.
Regt/Corps ........... stationed in the Camp Area  is
                                    *
authorised to enter Camps 1 / 2/ 3 and Hospital Block on duty.

Date of issue 29.24.May45.                      Capt
                                          Colonel
Signature of holder Anita Lasker  Commander
                                          102 Control Section

NB   No person will enter any of the above unless fully
     protected by Typhus Innoculation and dusted with AL Powder
     prior to entry.

*  Delete where applicable.
```

Belsen, May 1945. A pass issued by the Military Government which gave me privileges as an interpreter

Renate was now a fully-fledged interpreter, and she had told me one day that the army were searching for anybody who could make themselves useful. I had offered my services in whatever capacity might be suitable. I had become an 'official interpreter' attached to the British Army, and been given an armband with 'I' for interpreter to wear. I must have been the first interpreter ever to have been unable to speak the language she was supposed to interpret. My main job at the beginning was to sit in an office and copy out various official reports on a typewriter. That was doubly funny because I couldn't really type either. I still can't: just with two fingers, but at a reasonable speed. I didn't understand a word of what I was copying and I read everything phonetically. However, I heard a lot of English being spoken all day long, and I somehow picked it up very quickly. In time I found myself both reading and understanding the texts I was copying. But I was skating on thin ice all the same. My lack of knowledge of English was not generally known and, since I wore the armband, I was often called on to sort out something. I became a master of improvisation. Of course knowing French made a difference. I don't think I caused any serious damage.

There was a great deal of looting in the early days after the liberation. I admit that I joined one of the looting parties myself one day, though I found the experience far from exhilarating. I remember finding myself in a house belonging to some Germans, the general idea being to help oneself to whatever took one's fancy. There was a child in the house who looked at me with total incomprehension. It made me realize that a thief is a thief

Telegram of 11th June 1945 to Harry Goldschmidt about our failure to get entry permits to England

whatever the circumstances. I left without touching a thing. There could never be adequate compensation for the losses we had sustained. Looting was not the answer.

Our day-to-day existence gradually fell into a kind of routine. I worked in the office; my English steadily improved. Of the good friends we made among our liberators I remember with special affection Chris Warner, who was most concerned about our personal safety. He fixed strong locks on the doors in our interpreter's house. It was Chris who made me a present of that grey army-typewriter box to house my belongings. He painted my initials on it. It was my 'suitcase' when I finally travelled to England. I still have it. In that box I found all the letters that have been so useful in compiling this book.

Our worries about establishing where we were to go and how we might organize going anywhere at all, grew daily. We were in touch with our relatives and everyone had offered us hospitality. But how to translate these offers into action was another matter. Europe was in turmoil. Immigration policy was not a priority anywhere. My cousin Jack, who was British, made several applications to the Home Office asking for permission for us to come to England, and so did Marianne and various other

people as well. The replies were always negative. There was no appara-
tus to deal with people like us. We were that new species, Displaced
Persons; and, let's face it, we were something of an embarrassment all
round.

Fortunately we had an occupation that kept our minds off our frus-
trating predicament. Apart from finding a home, my most overpowering
desire now was to get hold of a cello. Several members of HM Forces had
been trying hard to discover one for me. It was quite a task since looting
had become illegal. I had anyhow felt strongly that a cello taken from a
fellow cellist was not acceptable, even if he had stolen it himself. (I had
once been the proud owner of a beautiful cello made by Ventapane. God
knows who plays on it now.) Eventually my dream came true. One day
Capt Powell located a cello that was sitting on top of a cupboard in some
burgomaster's office. It did not seem to have an official owner. I found it
lying on my bed when I came back to my room one morning:

Belsen Camp, Sunday, 17th June 1945

My beloved M,

I am writing in a hurry because I am horrendously excited.

This morning I came back to our room after having breakfast with
Renate, and what did I see lying on my bed? Just lying on my bed??

You may have three guesses … It is Sunday again: my third lucky
Sunday.

The first was the day of *liberation* on 15th April.

The second was when *your first letter* came on 20th May.

And the third Sunday is today: 17th June.

Have you guessed?

I HAVE GOT A CELLO

It was given to me by the senior officer I have told you about. He knew
that I played the cello and he gave me this surprise today.

I am absolutely speechless. He has been pestering all the mayors he can
in Hamburg, Hanover and other towns around and about.

Yes, I am a 'Sunday luck child'. That is clear as mud. And what is more,
it is a good cello and makes a good sound. Marianne, I am going half
crazy!!!

As soon as you can please send me some *strings, A, D, G, and C,* some
'rosin' (I think that is the English word) and also the music I have already
asked for. If you get the strings and the rosin before you find the music,
please send them separately. Don't wait until you have got everything.

The cello does have strings, but they are badly worn and I have to be very careful with them. I am jumping up and down with impatience. My cello is smiling at me from the corner of the room.

My stiff fingers badly need scales. So here I go … Write soon. Thanks for everything.

Yours … Anita

I was over the moon. It was an early birthday present. But I was temporarily frustrated because I did not have any rosin, and it was impossible to get any sound from the cello. I forget what the remedy was. I soon started to scratch away, and news spread round the camp that I was 'operational' as a cellist again. That was far from the truth of course, but it didn't matter.

These two are from Renate:

Belsen Camp, 17th June 1945

Dearest Marianne,

We have just received your letter of 1st June. In time for Sunday breakfast. Your letters are always like a slice of home for me. I can see you here in the room … You ask me why I write so infrequently. I must tell you that I am interpreter to the Staff Captain and we go to Hamburg, Hanover and places in the area to obtain clothing for the camp every day. All the Germans in this district have to provide one complete outfit from their best clothing, and we fetch everything in a large lorry. That is how the people in the camp will soon be decently dressed. It is incredible how much has been achieved during these past few months. People are living in marvellous billets with proper sanitation; they are getting very good food; and they are being completely fitted out with new clothes. Half the camp is still closely fenced in to isolate the typhus hospitals where more than 12,000 people are being looked after by the English Red Cross. They are given fruit and vegetables, and books to read, and they are slowly changing back into human beings …

… Re

Belsen Camp, 19th June 1945

My dearest Marianne,

Four letters from you yesterday!!! What a lucky day … We watch the people here (who are all very kind to us) with rather pitiless eyes because there is one thing in particular that we have learned in the concentration camps: how to get to know people and judge them for their true worth. Most people who should have shown themselves to be human in the hour of need have turned out to be animals. I immediately visualize everybody we meet now as camp inmates and try to imagine how they would behave in such a situation ... Anita is indescribably happy with her cello. It is a beautiful instrument and she plays as beautifully as ever. Our friend who brought it for her can't stop looking at her happy face. I was determined that she should have it for her birthday and she in fact got it a month earlier ...

I must finish here ...

Yours Reh

Stationed at Belsen at that time was Lady Montgomery, a high-ranking officer in charge of 'entertainment', whom I have mentioned before. She was charming and became a good friend to us. One day, she sent for me and told me of a plan she had to get some concerts going. Apparently there were some musicians in a nearby Italian PoW camp. She wanted to find out more about it and asked me to go along with her.

We drove to the camp and there we met three extremely dishevelled-looking Italian soldiers. One of them was Giuseppe Selmi. We were talking with him (I think in French), and it transpired that he had been the principal cellist for Radio Rome before the war. The other two soldiers were a pianist and a singer. With a lot of good will and talent for improvisation we formed ourselves into a 'concert party', and performed all over the place in ex-prison camps. Eva Steiner, who had been a member of the Auschwitz Orchestra, and was a fine singer, joined the party. Our resources were pitifully limited, as you might imagine, but standards were different then. We had a really good time together. Selmi, or Beppino as he was generally known, became a close friend too. He was such a nice man, and he helped me a great deal with my cello-playing. He was after all a most accomplished cellist while I was merely a student who had never had an opportunity to study seriously. I still have the programme for one of these concerts. It was sent to me a few years ago by a soldier who had been to one of them. It was most touching. (See page 119.)

The cello Selmi had managed to get hold of was infinitely inferior to mine. That is saying something because my cello was not actually as good as it seemed at the time. It had seemed marvellous but it was in reality a pathetic box, and when I came to England with it and had my first proper cello lesson with William Pleeth, one of the first things he did was to find me a better cello. He told me mine was utterly useless. However, as I have said, our standards in Belsen were not so demanding. Everything is relative, and my cello was that much less terrible than Selmi's. When he played his solos, I always let him use my cello. One of our party pieces was a Bach cello sonata arranged for two cellos.

The Italian members of our concert party were much less well off materially than we – the ex-Belsen prisoners – were. In fact, Selmi had virtually nothing apart from the shabby clothes he stood up in, which had been his uniform. He was not exactly presentable. One must remember that the Italians had changed sides during the war. They had fought with the Germans to start with, and only became their enemy later on. So when their prison camps were liberated they did not receive much help from their liberators, not least because they had never been reduced to the state we had. I was wealthy by comparison and was in the position of being able to supply poor old Selmi with such luxuries as socks and underwear. He was immensely grateful and assured me that he would never forget what I had done for him.

All this would perhaps be scarcely worth recording had it not been for another remarkable coincidence that took place some thirty-two years later.

My son Raphael had won first prize in the Cassado Competition which had taken place in Florence. He then played with the orchestra there on occasion, and got to know its members sufficiently well to notice, when he returned to Florence the following year to play the Schumann Concerto, that a different principal cellist was sitting in the orchestra, and he introduced himself. The cellist was none other than Giuseppe Selmi, who lived in Rome but had been called in to deputize for this concert in Florence. He had had no idea whom he was going to play with in Florence. When he heard my son's name, and realized that the young man was the son of Anita - of Belsen concert-party, socks and underwear fame - a veritable explosion took place. Selmi was – since he died a few years ago – an ebullient man in spite of his advanced years. He became terribly excited. The whole orchestra was compelled to gather around him and hear the story of our meeting so long ago. I am told that total chaos followed and that the performance was extremely emotional, especially the cello duet in the slow movement.

I saw Selmi some years afterwards in Rome. We had a wonderful evening together, reminiscing and marvelling at the lucky chance that took him to Florence for my son's concert and brought us together again. He told me that when he realized who the soloist was, he had had the sensation that his blood was ebbing away, and had nearly fainted.

Back to 1945 and my life in Belsen. Essentially, it was a period of waiting and endlessly fantasizing about what 'real life' was going to be like once we had succeeded in getting out. Marianne finally had the opportunity to emigrate to Palestine, as it still was, and so we were presented with a dreadful dilemma. There was not yet any possibility of our being able to leave Belsen and go to England, and the problem was this: should Marianne wait for us and run the risk of missing her chance to emigrate, or should she go and consign our reunion to the distant future. I wrote to her on 19th June 1945 (this is a continuation of the letter about my parents' deportation):

... I now come to another point in your letter on which I would like to elaborate: I admit that the first few days after the liberation were like a dream, and everything English was sacred and holy. But that was just the beginning. Now we have got both feet on the ground again, and I must reassure you ... We have acquired damned sharp eyesight. If you have witnessed the greatest degradation on earth, you become very critical. Yes, I often wish I could be less critical because I am always having to bite my tongue hard so as not to be rude.

And last but not least: you – us – and our future. I did write asking you to wait for us ... But you shouldn't think for one minute that that is what we really want. All personal considerations must be switched off ... I know we will see each other again soon. You should be aware of one thing, which is important for your well-being: *we are not the least bit impatient*!!!!!!!!!!!!

We know how difficult everything is ... Please write and tell us frankly exactly when you are intending to leave ... Love and greetings ...

Signed: Titel and Reh

PS I am full of admiration for your ability to speak fluent Hebrew, Marianne. Perhaps you won't look down on us with too much disdain if we tell you that we have learned to speak fluent French. If Hélène doesn't write soon we will get completely out of the habit, and so we have decided to speak French to one another. We hear enough English, and we may quietly forget our German. Amen! I'll finish here. I ought to put in an occasional appearance in the office.

Yes, my birthday is approaching. The second 0 in my life. What I long for above all, that is, if it is remotely possible – even if you have to commit theft – is to have some good pictures of our parents and of home ... I know we will have to be patient. In other ways I have been trying to be as demanding as I can. So far I have not succeeded. That has less to do with my inborn modesty than with the fact that we are happy with what we have – and we have everything we need except the one *major* thing. But we are keeping up our hopes, and if you hope and wish very hard, you bring down fulfilment from heaven. I am speaking from experience ... 'Be strong and of good courage.'

Yours A

The traumas of achieving entry to England
I wrote this:

Belsen Camp, 25th June 1945

My dearest M ...

Yesterday evening I was playing on my sad three remaining strings when Cpl Shott came in with your greetings ... I need hardly tell you of my – or rather our – joy ... What you told him about your life made a deep impression and as I listened to him I was filled with wonder that there can be such totally different lives beneath the same sky ... Marianne, you must be very happy, and that makes me happy too. I am beginning to understand the world situation, and this morning I was given the *Jewish Chronicle* ... Its main topic is 'The Jewish Problem', and yes, I am beginning to understand ... Among other items in the paper, it said that 1000 children will be getting permission to come to England. What do you think about that? I don't know whether there are 'people in charge of this' over here, or whether we should be expecting somebody. Today I am having a meeting with Lady Montgomery. Although she is really too official a person to work for individuals, I shall do my utmost to squeeze all I can out of her. The most difficult thing to stomach is that we are *German* Jews. I cannot possibly express what an effect this has on me. If I had not taken a vow after the liberation to conduct myself like a half-civilized person, I would pick up the various ink-pots that surround me and hurl them against the wall, or else relieve myself in some other unlady-like fashion. But I have acquired a large stomach and have managed to swallow even the fact that I am a German Jew, although it stuck in my throat and I can't see how I will be able to come to terms with it ... Many thousand thanks for the music. It is a pity so much is out of print ...

My God, I must have fallen on my head. I've just remembered that my greatest joy has been the photographs. I carry them around with me wherever I go and show them to every victim who falls into my hands. I am so happy to have them. From time to time Renate snatches them from me, and then we look at them together and cannot agree which of us should take them ...

With all my love, Yours Anita

This letter was from Renate:

Belsen Camp, 5th July 1945

... I should tell you that the Jewish Mission has come here now. The Rabbi has told us that in about four weeks a transport of about 1000 young people is probably going to be sent to Palestine via England, and that we ought to be the first names on the list. Wouldn't that be marvellous? ... We saw the Jewish newspaper where Anita's BBC statement was printed, and also an article by you. We are very proud of our famous sister.

Yesterday Anita played in front of a public audience for the first time after such ages, a Bach sonata for cello and piano. It was beautiful and everybody liked it. Afterwards, we had an incredible dinner served by two waiters. There was so much cutlery we did not know where to start. Understandably, since during the past four years we only had a spoon and even that was a precious possession. To begin with we had nothing at all and gobbled the smelly turnip soup from tin bowls.

I can still see Anita sitting in front of that stinking stew, unable to touch it until hunger compelled her to drink it like the rest of us. This week I am going to Hamburg to find a nice birthday present for Titel. She will be twenty and I am sure Vati would have thought of something special ... I wish you lots of luck in your new country and kiss you a thousand times.

Renate

And here are more letters from both of us:

Belsen Camp, 7th July 1945

Dearest M,

... It is reassuring to know that so much is being done for us in Palestine too. I am hoping against hope that one day our dreams will become reality ... Your parcel with A string, cigarette-case and the absolutely A1 rosin arrived in first-class condition. Many, many thanks. Soon it will be Mutti's birthday. We will try and get hold of a memorial candle. And should this letter reach you before the 20th, we will think of one another hard that day ...

Quick, quick, a letter from you ... Your loving

Anita

Belsen Camp, 16th July 1945

Dearest Marianne,

... We have nothing new to report. Morale is good and we are still hoping that in the end everything will turn out for the best. We are pinning our hopes on the children's transport, and we receive daily promises that every attempt will be made to squeeze us in, in spite of our age. The projected transport is for children up to sixteen. As there are not enough children of that age available, we might be included as 'guardians'.

Tomorrow is Tita's birthday. Our friend Capt Powell and I made a special trip to Hamburg yesterday to buy her some presents. She will be getting blouses, underwear, shoes, two dresses and a fantastic birthday cake made from sixteen eggs, and also chicken, cherries and ice-cream. Amazing isn't it? My only worry now is where to find her a cello case. I could not track one down anywhere in Hamburg as all the instrument-makers have been bombed out. I think I will have to get one made by the dressmaker. Oh yes, she will be having twenty little candles on her cake. I am so glad that I can do all this for her on her first birthday in freedom ... Anita is sitting opposite me and painting posters for the office ... I must close and return to my 'hard work'. Don't worry, I am not doing too much. When I was so sick it was not because of my work but because my heart was a bit shaky after the typhus, and also it is very hot here at the moment.

Write soon ... Yours Renate

Belsen Camp, 16th July 1945

My dearest M,

... Today is the last day I'll be nineteen. My age will never again start with a '1' (unless I live to 100). I am unhappy about this because I am really quite old now. Yesterday evening we went to a Robert Taylor film, and I noticed how old we have become. I remember him as a young and handsome youth and now he is a grown man. Isn't it terrible how life races by? I have a good mind to try and tether it. I am playing the cello a lot and my hands tremble when I do because I am unused to it.

Tomorrow, a marvellous Italian cellist, an 'ex-prisoner-of-war', is coming here to give a concert ... As long as he is in Belsen I will take lessons with him. I can scarcely wait. Last week I went with Lady Montgomery to his camp, which is an hour's drive from here, and he played for me. Absolutely beautifully ... The paper is at an end. Till next time ...

Your still nineteen-year-old Anita

Belsen Camp, 23rd July 1945

Dearest Marianne,

I've just received the letter you wrote on the boat ... I can well understand how impressed you must have been by Vesuvius and all the other sights. I cried with laughter at your description of the posh life on board and your attempts at dancing. I admit I am a bit envious. No, that's not true, I simply admire you for having made it and for having finally fulfilled your wish. Anita and I are praying that we don't have to wait too long for a reunion.

Helli has written us a rather discouraging letter. The Home Office told them that they can apply again in three months' time, but we are still hoping that the children's transport will set off one day – perhaps.

Cultural life is really picking up. Tomorrow for instance we will have Yehudi Menuhin here and we are very excited about it ... We had a nice birthday celebration for Anita. All the parcels arrived in time, and thanks to Capt Powell I got everything I wanted ... The only items missing are a winter coat and some pullovers, but I am sure we will be able to find those as well ... So we are ready to go!! ... I have just heard that our chances of joining the children's transport are good and that it may leave at the beginning of August ... Oh, if only that were true! I would go mad with joy ...   [Renate]

Belsen, July 1945

Darling M,

... Our future still seems very uncertain. Now that the elections have turned out so fantastically well, we are a little more hopeful as far as England is concerned ... We fervently hope that something will happen soon because we are really just hanging around. The Pioneer Corps has left, and Capt Powell, our best friend, will be leaving before long, too, as he is being discharged from the army. We are going to be very lonely ...

Greetings to all our friends ...

Yours Re

PROGRAMMA

PARTE PRIMA

Violoncello:

Schumann - Träumerei .... Anita Lasker

Selmi - La citta del sogno dai campanili dorati .... Giuseppe Selmi

Piano solo:

Mendelssohn - Rondo capriccioso ....,..... Giorgio Perrini

Canto:

Giordano - Andrea Chenier - Nemico della patria ....: G. Gaudioso

Puccini - Boheme - Mi chiamano Mimi. .... Eva Steiner

Maggioli - Na stella .... Gerardo Gaudioso

Puccini - Madama Butterfly - Un bel di vedremo .... Eva Steiner

PARTE SECONDA

Piano solo:

Beethoven - Sonata patetica ....:...... Giorgio Perrini

Violoncello solo:

Selmi - Giuochi di bimbi nel giardino -

    Fischer - Danza ungherese .... Giuseppe Selmi

Canto: ˈ

Tosti - L'ultima canzone .... Gerardo Gaudioso

Piano solo:

Chopin - La caduta di Varsavia........................ Giorgio Perrini

Violoncello:

Bach - Sonata per due violoncelli .... Anita Lasker e Giuseppe Selmi

Canto:

Leoncavallo - Mattinata .... Eva Steiner

Bizet - Carmen - Con voi ber .... Gerardo Gaudioso

Delibes - Les filles de Cadiz.... .... Eva Steiner

Belsen, July 1945. Programme for a concert given by the group of musicians assembled by Lady
Montgomery to entertain Displaced Persons' camps

Belsen Camp, 30th July 1945

My dearest H [Helli]

... On Friday Yehudi Menuhin was here in Belsen Camp. At first it seemed as if this concert was going to be 'for Poles only', and we were really furious, but it then transpired that it was not meant literally and we got tickets without any trouble.

It was a wonderful evening. Both soloist and accompanist were dressed in simple attire bordering on the slovenly, which matched the surroundings perfectly. It goes without saying that Menuhin played faultlessly; he is after all Yehudi Menuhin. But I must confess (and please don't take this as impertinence on my part) that I was a little disappointed. His playing didn't have the soul that I imagine Casals' has. I had the distinct impression that he was saving himself. It could well be that he did not find the atmosphere very inspiring. For it was impossible to get complete silence in the hall, and I was thoroughly ashamed of the audience. In fact it was amazing that he did not just stop in midstream.

As for his accompanist, I can only say that I cannot imagine anything done more beautifully. He was completely unobtrusive and yet I found myself transfixed by him sitting there as if he wouldn't say boo to a goose – but playing to perfection. [The accompanist was none other than Benjamin Britten, it emerged later.]

Yes, who would ever have believed that Belsen Camp would hear Yehudi Menuhin playing? By the way, he played the Bach/Kreisler Prelude and Fugue, the *Kreutzer Sonata*, Mendelssohn's Concerto, something by Debussy and several smaller, unfamiliar items.

About the two of us, I realize that Jack's letter to Capt Powell doesn't look too hopeful. Is that really a point of contention: 'German-born refugees'?! Yes, of course we will continue to set our sights on the children's transport, but as our only hope it seems rather insubstantial. When, oh when will all these problems finally be resolved? When will we be free to do what we want? We are not ungrateful and we appreciate the freedom we now have ... But that is no longer my main concern. Last week, when I was together with some musicians, especially a cellist, I became aware how infinitely much I still have to learn. Selmi has given me lots of advice, and within certain limits I can work by myself. But it is those limits that depress me so much. These days spent rushing between office and cello are lost days. Since I had my twentieth birthday, I can almost *hear* myself getting older and older without being where I would so wish to be, that

is at a music school and not in the *office of the chief clerk, Belsen Camp*. I
know that everything humanly possible is being done and I do appreciate it. We are a thousand times better off than everyone else. It is the
waiting and waiting that saps my strength, and the fighting against a
thousand idiotic difficulties, even if they are understandable ...

   The election results made me very happy. Will this improve things for
us unfortunate 'refugees'? ... We have heard again from Palestine. It
doesn't seem as if we are short of homes. That is a consolation ... And
please, I gave an A string to Selmi yesterday because his had broken. Could
you get hold of another one for me? ... Keep well ...

Yours Anita

Belsen Camp, 10th August 1945

My beloved M,

   It is raining, raining, raining ... Typical Belsen weather. I have just been
practising, and the reason I have stopped is that I am exhausted through
and through. Everything hurts. Yes, getting rid of six years of stiffness is
a tough job. I was with Selmi for the last time today. He is returning to
Rome ... He has left me a whole book of exercises, and that'll be a real
sweat. It is a total mystery how I have ever been able to play anything
from beginning to end without dropping my bow. If you gather from all
this cello gossip that I am not interested in anything else at the moment
then you are – to be absolutely honest – partly right. My desire to study
properly again – at last – is getting more overpowering every day, and as
a result Belsen is getting on my nerves more and more.

   ... I have just realized that you haven't heard how my birthday went
... Helli's parcels all arrived on the dot on the 17th. Your greetings, for
which I thank you a thousand times, came a few days later. My birthday
spread was fabulous. A fantastic cake with twenty candles was the first
thing that caught my eye. And then from Helli there were lovely slippers,
cream, a chess game, silk underwear, shoes, a dress and a host of smaller
things too numerous to mention. One of my main presents was of course
the cello, which I had in advance. Now I've really reached the ripe old
age of twenty, and feel geriatric. But I suppose there's nothing to be done
about that ... I'll close now and give my fossilized fingers another run-
around.

   I embrace you a thousand times with all my love,

Yours Anita

Belsen Camp, 29th August 1945

My beloved M,

    ... You have not heard from us for a long time and I can do nothing but ask for your forgiveness and patience. For some weeks I have been incapable of writing ... I don't want to talk much about this place here, for the worlds we live in are too different, and what could be said would be too long-winded to write down.

    I just want to thank you for your letters. The happiness that radiates from them helps cheer us up for hours. You have also given us a lot of hope in connection with the certificates. Up to now there has never been anything like a private certificate but perhaps, perhaps, it will be possible to obtain one all the same!!!!! It is high time for us to get out of here ...

    Do you read the papers? Because I have written an article – and I think it will be published either in the *Jewish Chronicle* or the *New Statesman,* or in the *Daily Mirror* – as a reply to a piece that appeared in the *Daily Express* about Germany's 'Gayest Holiday Town', its name 'Belsen' ... The thought of another Belsen winter fills me with horror. Keep well, and don't be gloomy even if I am. Be as happy as you are for ever ...

    Love from

Your Anita

This was from Renate:

Belsen Camp, 30th August 1945

Dearest Marianne,

    ... Yes, we are still in 'beautiful' Belsen ... Your latest letters have been so full of promises of certificates about to be obtained that they made us go quite crazy. We had resigned ourselves to sitting here for at least another six months, even though the prospect was extremely distasteful. I know that a lot of applications *have* been made from England ... You will understand, Marianne, that we are sick and tired of the camp. It gets worse every day. It is terribly overcrowded. Thank God we live in our little house by ourselves ... The whole atmosphere is so depressing, I cannot stand looking at all those faces any more ...

... R

We made many good friends among the Relief Teams, and life was not entirely humdrum. There was, for instance, the occasion when I heard that ENSA (the Entertainment National Service Association) was coming to Hamburg with a performance of *Figaro* conducted by Walter Süsskind. It was meant for army personnel of course. At that time I was working for a certain Lt Winchester and he knew what it would mean to me if I could go and hear the opera. He suggested that he should take me along – stretching the definition of 'army personnel' somewhat – provided that I could organize some sort of uniform for myself. That seemed reasonably easy, and I planned to don the uniform of a member of the Jewish Relief Team for the occasion. When the day came, however, complications arose. The person who was going to lend me her uniform was nowhere to be found, and it seemed as if the whole enterprise was doomed to failure. But not a bit of it.

I think it was Joe Wollhandler from UNRRA (the United Nations Relief and Rehabilitation Agency) who was determined that I should not be disappointed, and a uniform was produced just in time. There was only one snag: it was that of a very high-ranking Red Cross officer with an impressive number of pips on its shoulders, and there was no headgear to go with it. But who cares about such minor details? I donned the uniform and, as you might imagine, looked utterly ridiculous. The disparity between my face and my 'rank' screamed to high heaven. Off we went to Hamburg and I enjoyed the outing no end. But the impressions that have stayed with me all these years are not so much artistic ones as those I had of the total devastation of Hamburg. Nothing had yet been cleared up.

The streets were littered with debris, and driving was an obstacle race. What a senseless waste! I have no idea whether the performance was good. I had no criteria for judging it. But it was all very exciting. At one point I suddenly realized that I had to face another problem. I would have quite liked to go to the loo, but I did not dare to. I did not want to find myself in a confined space right next to somebody from 'my unit'. I must have survived somehow. We got back to Belsen unscathed. The uniform was duly returned, without its owner ever knowing where it had been.

Belsen Camp, 23rd September 1945

Dearest M,

... In the past few days the following things have happened: On Wednesday afternoon I went to Hamburg disguised as a Red Cross officer ... At 1 a.m. I was back in Belsen, and at 7 a.m. I went to Lüneburg as a 'witness' in the Belsen trial … In the evening, when the court adjourned, I tore back to Belsen illegally because I had given a holy, holy promise not to let down the evening performance of the Jewish Theatre.

Next morning at 7 a.m. I was in the car again heading for Lüneburg with the 'Jewish Brigade'. Of course we had a puncture, and I only made it to the court with minutes to spare. Thank God my absence went unnoticed. Now I am back in Belsen again because we have the weekend off, but in half-an-hour I must set out again. There is nothing to tell you about Lüneburg yet. I have not yet 'given evidence' but I am counting on doing that this week. More soon …

Yours Anita

It was September, and the Lüneburg trial that I mentioned in my letter was the next big distraction from the endless waiting for the end to our domicile in Belsen. I was called as a witness. The trial struck me as a huge farce. I came face to face with British justice, under which you are innocent unless proven guilty, for the first time. This is no doubt a commendable principle, but it is difficult to apply or even adapt to the sort of crimes that were being dealt with in Lüneburg. I saw them there all lined up: Kramer (the Belsen Camp Commander), Klein (a doctor), Grese, the lot, and with them, admittedly at the end of the line, some of the Kapos who had distinguished themselves by their bestial behaviour towards their fellow prisoners.

My command of the English language was reasonably good by then and I was able to dispense with an interpreter. First, I had to identify the prisoners. That was easy enough. (I wonder what went through Kramer's head when I identified him?) Then came the absurd aspect of the proceedings. For example, there were questions like: ' … did you ever see any of these people kill anybody? … ' If you answered 'yes', the next question would be: 'which day of the week was this, and what time exactly?' Naturally you had to answer 'I don't know'. You were under oath, but in the camp you had neither a watch nor a calendar, nor would you have been the slightest bit interested whether it was Monday or Tuesday. That you simply could not answer such a question was enough to make you feel you were not telling the truth. It was hard for me to reconcile myself to the fact that these criminals actually had a counsel for their defence, just as in a normal British law court. That made me very angry indeed. So angry that I said there and then, in the witness box and under oath, that, while I was not defending the Kapos, I thought it entirely

KLEIN SAID AT BELSEN 'NOW WE SHALL BE KIND'

The British were on their way

From NORMAN CLARK
News Chronicle Special Correspondent

LUNEBURG, Monday.

A FEW days before the British liberated Belsen, S.S. Guards in the camp, including Dr. Fritz Klein—No. 2 prisoner in the war crimes trial here —began wearing Red Cross armlets.

Klein told the starving inmates of the camp : " We shall now be kind to the sick among you ; we shall treat you all well."

Irma Grese, senior superintendent at Belsen, told 19-year-old German political prisoner Anita Lasker, niece of the world chess player Dr. Lasker : " We shall all be liberated soon."

Grese then tried to "mix" with the prisoners.

It was Anita who gave the Court these sidelights on the last days of Belsen.

Gas chamber queues

At Auschwitz camp she played the cello in the camp orchestra, she said in evidence, and had quarters within sight of the crematorium.

" So many people were sent to the camp," she added, " that every night there was a queue waiting to enter the gas chamber."

A Rumanian doctor from Paris, Sigismund Bendel, who, as a prisoner in Auschwitz, worked in the crematorium, told the Court of scenes in the gas chambers when the ghetto of Lodz, in Poland, was liquidated, with the extermination of 80,000 Jews.

Victims fought

Of what happened when the doors of the gas chamber were finally locked against the struggling wall of victims, the witness said : " One hears cries and shouts. They start to fight each other. They beat on the walls. This goes on for four minutes. Then there is complete silence—nothing more.

" Five minutes later the doors are opened, but not until another quarter of an hour has passed has the gas dispersed sufficiently for the special working party of prisoners to enter the chamber and start the work of dragging out the bodies.

" When the doors are opened bodies, piled 5ft. high, compressed and interlocked, fall out."

Like devils

He told of the work of the special working parties of prisoners whose task it was to remove the dead from the gas chambers and carry them to the crematorium or the incinerator pits.

" All hell is let loose. These special working parties work with a mad fury. They are no longer human. They are like devils.

" As they strive to work faster blows from sticks and truncheons are rained on them by S.S. overseers. People it was impossible to get into the gas chamber are continuously being shot beside trenches, which were dug as burning pits, because the crematorium was not adequate to dispose of all the bodies."

Of 11,000 gipsies in the camp to which Dr. Bendel was sent first at Auschwitz 4,300 were sent to the crematorium in a month. Systematic extermination of gipsies was practised.

Orchestra of death played at gaol camp

A NITA LASKER, a German Jewess, told the Belsen court yesterday that an orchestra had to play at the gates of Auschwitz gaol camp as lorries drove in with people destined for the gas chamber.

Frau Lasker, aged ——— was a member of the orchestra. She said she was arrested in Breslau for helping French prisoners to escape.

It was the thirteenth day of the trial of Kramer and his forty-four associates and Lasker identified several prisoners, including Irma Grese.

She told how arrivals at Auschwitz became so numerous that there was a queue for the crematorium.

When the British were near Belsen the SS guards put on Red Cross armlets.

It was announced yesterday that a search for the mass graves as yet undiscovered is to begin at Belsen, following the disclosure that 40,000 internees are still missing.

October 1945. Newspaper reports in the British press about the trial in Lüneburg, mentioning the evidence I gave

IRMA CONFESSION STAYS SECRET

Belsen men hanged in pairs

From MONTAGUE LACEY: Herford, Friday

THE death cell confessions and last statements of Josef Kramer, Beast of Belsen, Irma Greese and the nine other Nazi men and women hanged yesterday at Hamelin, city of the Pied Piper, are being checked today by British military prison officials.

It is unlikely that any of them will ever be made public.

Official notices of the executions are being sent to the relatives of the executed, and military government notices that the sentences have been carried out are being published in all German newspapers.

The 11 hangings took place in secrecy stricter even than in a British jail.

Pierrepoint, the British hangman, brought specially to Germany, carried out all the sentences in six hours and 19 minutes, helped by his assistant, British Military Police and German prison officials.

The prisoners were warned before breakfast that their last hour had come. A number asked to see the German prison chaplain.

Twenty-six-year-old Elizabeth Volkenrath, chief of the S.S. women guards at the Belsen concentration camp, was hanged first at 9.34 a.m.

QUIETLY

Blonde, 22-year-old Irma Greese, and witch-like 52-year-old Juana Borman, the "woman with the dog," followed at half-hour intervals.

By 10.38 a.m. all the women had been executed. They went quietly and quickly to the scaffold, their arms pinioned behind them.

Then, in a break of nearly two hours, the execution shed was prepared for the double hanging of the eight men, and at 12.11 p.m. Kramer, the big, brute-like camp commandant, and Fritz Klein, 58-year-old camp doctor, who made the selections for the gas chamber, were hanged side by side.

Thirty-five minutes later another pair was executed. Then there was a break until 3.37 p.m., when Pichen and Hoessler were executed.

At 4.16 p.m., when Wilhelm Dorr and Franz Dtofel went through the trapdoor, there ended the terrible story of Belsen, where thousands of men and women were murdered.

Extraordinary precautions were taken to prevent any sort of demonstration outside the jail, but it was all unnecessary, as, apart from those inside, none knew that the hangings were taking place.

October 1945. Newspaper report in the British press about the execution of Josef Kramer, Irma Grese, Elisabeth Volkenrath, Juana Bormann, Fritz Klein, Franz Hoessler and other German personnel who ran Belsen Camp

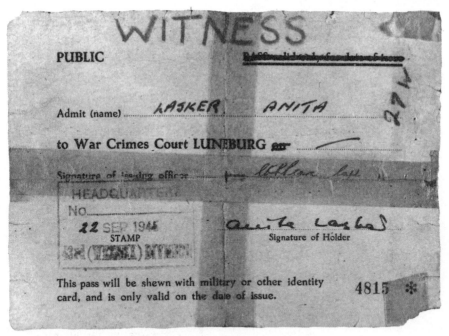

My witness card for the Lüneburg trial

wrong that they should be tried alongside the people whose system had turned them into the animals they had become. The Kapos should have had their own separate trial. However, it had no noticeable effect. Most of the defendants were sentenced to death anyway. The whole trial was, as it happened, a wonderful opportunity for a lot of young barristers to display their ability to defend criminals. It was sick-making for the likes of us who had been at the receiving end of this murder machine. (See Appendix 4 on page 157.)

It was at that instant that I understood for the first time how incomprehensible to the rest of the world were the events which had led to the Lüneburg Trial. Is it possible to apply *law* in the conventional sense to crimes so far removed from the law as the massacre of millions of people, which were perpetrated in the cause of 'purifying the human race'?

Renate wrote these two letters to Marianne:

Belsen Camp, 29th September 1945

Dearest M,

... this week a Jewish Congress has started here. But I think all this is just a lot of bullshit and I didn't listen to their endless talks. Three MPs were here and gave boring speeches ... Our chances of going to England don't look too bad at present ... Anita is still in Lüneburg at the War Crimes Trial and I am running the office all by myself. I am driving there this afternoon to fetch her back for the weekend. I am very lonely without her and happy when she comes home for a day and a half ...

Yours Renate

Belsen Camp, 2nd October 1945

Dearest M ...

You write such beautiful letters. We read them over and over again ... It is very depressing that so many obstacles are being put in our way in trying to find a home for ourselves ... Titel is in Lüneburg again ... People are writing a good deal about her in the papers and talking about her on the radio ... She has made a plan of the layout of the camp which has been printed and given to all the members of the High Court, much to the irritation of the 'defending officers', as many of the details of certain buildings are highly incriminating for the accused ...

Yours Re

I wrote this to my cousin Helli after my court appearance:

Lüneburg, 2nd October 1945

Dearest H,

It is all over now, and I shall have a bitter after-taste for a long time to come. It was not so much that one had to see these criminal types again and that one felt transported back into the past. I stood there, and I was asked questions, and as far as I am concerned I answered them more briefly and to the point than may have been strictly necessary. However much I racked my brain to describe things in greater detail and more effectively, I just could not do it in this overblown theatre. I spoke in English which made a great impression, although what the witnesses looked like seemed to be of greater interest to these gentlemen than what they had to say. The *Daily Mirror* photographed me in a variety of poses ...

It was during the trial, when I was sitting in the canteen having a cup of tea, that a young man came towards me. It turned out to be my old friend Konrad Latte, the very man who had supplied me with the cyanide he had subsequently replaced with icing-sugar. He had read reports of the

Konrad Latte ~~Beier~~
Kapellmeister

~~Bad Homburg v. d. H.,~~ den S. X. 194 5

Anita,
Du lebst — es ist kaum zu fassen. Telegrafiere mir bitte sofort, ob und wo ich Dich erreichen kann — ich kann überall hinkommen.

Dein K.

Later,
Hamm Westfalen
Soester str. 184
Tel. 1949

October 1945. Letter from my friend Konrad Latte who gave me the 'poison' that turned out to be icing-sugar. 'You are alive. It is inconceivable. Cable me immediately and tell me if and where I can find you. I can go anywhere.'

trial in the papers and had seen my name mentioned. It was an amazing reunion. Konrad himself had managed to hide and survive against incredible odds. One of the first things I said to him — casually — was: 'Thanks for the sugar. I enjoyed it.' But for his intuition we would not have had this conversation ...

And this to Marianne:

Belsen Camp, 19th October 1945

My dearest M,

... Things have been quite eventful in the meantime. I don't know whether you read the English papers. If you do, you will have seen that Anita Lasker 'a young German Jewess' gave evidence at the Lüneburg Belsen trial. The trial is still not finished, and since I have to be in Lüneburg every day but return to Belsen in between, I am only half here and half there at the moment.

In Lüneburg I had a telegram from somebody who had read about me in the press and found out that I was still alive. This somebody was ... Konrad Latte!!!! He came to Lüneburg immediately and, improbable though it may sound after *these* three years which we have both lived through, we just continued where we had left off. We kept on asking each other whether it was really possible that we were sitting there as if nothing had happened and talking as if we had just parted company. Konrad had lived all that time illegally in the most demeaning conditions: he had been arrested, and had escaped ... It is difficult to comprehend how life can go on despite everything. Konrad's parents are no longer alive.

I'll write again soon about this and other things.

... Yours Anita

Back in England, my family and friends kept bombarding the Home Office for permission for us to come to England. It looked fairly hopeless ... Although Britain had won the war, life there was still far from normal. In fact it took many years for normality to return. The Home Office had other things to think about apart from creating machinery to allow Displaced Persons to come and live in their country.

Finally, it was the end of November 1945 by then, a bill was passed in Parliament to the effect that Displaced Persons would be allowed to join their relatives in England provided they were under the age of twenty-one and had no relatives anywhere else in the world. If they met these conditions, they were to report to their nearest British Passport Control Office. Jack and Helli were told about this new and very welcome development, and passed what they had heard on to us.

We were absolutely delighted. I admit that I had forgotten until recently how desperate we had become by then to get out of Belsen and start a normal life. Nor had I been fully aware of the colossal efforts that were made to get us to England, not only by my immediate family but also by friends and well-wishers. The 1945 letters to Marianne brought it all back to me.

We were now faced with two minor problems: Renate had reached the antique age of twenty-one in January 1945, and was therefore over the age limit; and, as far as relatives outside the UK were concerned, there was of course uncle Edward in America. However, old combatants like us are not so easily deterred by such details. It took fifty NAAFI cigarettes to have our dates of birth altered at the Registry Office in Belsen. There was not a scrap of proof as to my identity anyway since I had no birth certificate. Actually, the whole operation suited me very well. I had lost so many years of my life, and I now was able to 'give myself back' two years. I never let on to anybody about this, not even my own children, until a few years ago when I made my 'confession'. Inevitably this false date of birth has brought about some peculiar situations. When I had my fiftieth birthday, I did not celebrate it specially because I was still only 'forty-eight'; and when I eventually had my fiftieth birthday party, I was already fifty-two. Also, I should have been able to claim my Free Bus Pass two years earlier, and other OAP advantages. But I have gained more than I have lost. Two years late, I finally got my Bus Pass, and I have long since given up caring about my age.

We had solved the problem of our ages. That left us with, first, the problem that our uncle Edward was living in the States, and, second, that we did not know how to get to the nearest British Passport Office – at a time when there was no official way of travelling. There were no trains, and above all there was no way you could cross frontiers. We had no papers, and certainly nothing as extravagant as a passport. The nearest Passport Office was in Brussels.

We did not give uncle Edward too much thought and concentrated on the main problem in hand: getting to Brussels. All our friends in the various Relief Units tried to find ways and means of helping us solve it. After a while, someone produced the following plan. Every month a lorry came all the way to Belsen from Brussels to deliver apples. We should organize some sort of uniform for ourselves to make us look a bit official, and then travel on the lorry when it returned to Brussels. It seemed a dubious proposition, but it was worth a try, we thought. It was December and very near Christmas, and that was probably the reason why we waited and waited and the lorry never came. We were extremely disappointed and rather depressed.

To cheer ourselves up, we accepted an invitation to the Officers' Club on Boxing Day. One of my first dancing partners was Hans Alexander, Capt Alexander to be correct. He knew about our urgent need to get to Brussels, and as we were dancing he said: 'I hear you want to go to Brussels. I am going there tomorrow. If you like, I'll take you along ...' Still dancing, I said to him: 'You know that we haven't got any papers ...' He replied: 'That is your problem. If you want to come, I'll pick you up around 8 o'clock in the morning.'

Well, well. That was quite an offer. It goes without saying that I accepted. It was like another cheap movie, but it really did happen like that. When the dance was over, I went off to tell Renate about this fantastic chance to get away – at last. We had a quick conference with some of our friends from the Relief Units who were at the party. We left the Club and removed ourselves to one of the offices. We had decided that we had better furnish ourselves with something looking as official as possible before setting out. So there I was again 'producing' a document. Old habits die hard! Except that this time I was not dabbling in forgery. Instead, I invented a document. Our situation had no precedent and there was only one thing we could do which was to *improvise*. What I did not know then was that Capt Alexander was not worried whether we had any papers or not. He had plans of his own, which he divulged to us later. I sat down in front of the typewriter and typed the following naïve certificate (the original is reproduced below):

C E R T T F I C A T E

ANITA LASKER

    The above mentioned ex-internee of Belsen Concentration Camp is authorized to travel? to Brussels in order to complete repatriation procedure. She is to report to the British Passport Control Officer at the British Embassy, Brussels. She is to travel in the custody of Capt. Alexander.

12-27-45   Hohne

Belsen, December 1945. The certificate I typed in the middle of the night on 26th December which was to get me over the Dutch frontier

Certificate

ANITA LASKER
The above mentioned ex-internee of Belsen Concentration Camp
is authorized to travell [*sic*] to Brussels in order to complete
repatriation procedure. She is to report to the British Passport
Control Officer at the British Embassy in Brussels.
She is to travel in the custody of Capt Alexander.

12-27-45   Hohne

'Hohne' was the name used for Belsen at that point. I don't know why.
All that was needed now was an official stamp and a signature.

The rubber stamps were locked up unfortunately. One of the girls from
the Relief Team said she did not think that it would be too much of a
problem to procure a stamp plus signature by the morning, and suggested
that we went back to our house and got our things together. We would
have the completed document by the morning. Sure enough, in the early
hours the document was back in my hands with a 'Mil Gov' stamp and
the signature of a certain Capt Hunt on it. God knows how they managed
to get this poor dear Capt Hunt to leave the party in the middle of the
night, unlock the stamp-drawer and sign his name. I think he must have
been pretty drunk.

Anyway, we were pleased with our combined handiwork and felt reasonably confident we would get by somehow. Quite laughable when you
consider that the 'document' was not typed on official paper, was written
in appalling English with spelling mistakes and was crowned with an unim-
pressive Military Government stamp. However, we were not too bothered
and all that was left for us to do was to wait for the arrival of Capt Alexander.
My luggage consisted of the old typewriter-case containing all my worldly
belongings and a cello.

We had some very anxious hours that morning of 27th December. Capt
Alexander had said he would pick us up first thing. We waited endlessly
but he failed to materialize. As time went by, we began to think that the
whole plan was a figment of our imagination. Finally he appeared around
lunchtime and was vaguely apologetic. (He has told me since that he got
very drunk the night before and overslept.)

We piled into the car, a chauffeur-driven Mercedes, and rolled out of
Belsen in style. We felt great. Capt Alexander never alluded to papers,

travel-passes or anything that might in any way be related to the fact that we were not exactly straightforward travelling-companions.

We drove towards Holland, and I enjoyed the ride until we got to the frontier. There we were promptly stopped and asked to show our papers. I tendered my home-made document to the guard and was not altogether surprised that he did not wave us on. We were politely asked to step out of the car and follow him. Once inside the guard-room he told us that as far as he was concerned Displaced Persons did not travel in private vehicles but only in large transports. He was very sorry but he could not let us pass. That was the cue for Capt Alexander. He took the papers out of the guard's hands – he outranked him naturally – looked at them for the first time and, without batting an eyelid, said brusquely: 'What's wrong with this! I have no time to hang around here. Put me on to HQ immediately!'

We had our reward for being collected so late in Belsen. It was already around 7 o'clock when we got to the frontier, and when he was at last connected to HQ, only a duty officer was available. Capt Alexander gave him a mouthful about being delayed without good reason. What could the wretched man on the other end of the line do but apologize and authorize the frontier guard to let us through?

Tense moments. I had seen myself being sent back to Belsen and having to start again from scratch.

As we were on Dutch soil, we went to a little restaurant to recover. I in turn apologized to Capt Alexander for having used his name on the paper. He just laughed. It was then that he told us he had only gone through with this charade for the hell of it. His plans for getting us over the frontier were as follows. He was a War Crimes Officer and it was his business to chase and arrest Nazis. If we had not succeeded in getting through at the first attempt, he would have driven on to another frontier post and taken us through as his prisoners. No one would have had the right to question him, or us. A most ingenious ruse; but I was glad we did not have to resort to it. It would have been somewhat preposterous to have had to pretend to be a war criminal in order to leave my 'fatherland'.

The next frontier was easy. That was the one between Holland and Belgium. Capt Alexander simply produced his papers and no questions were asked. By the time we reached Brussels it was midnight. Where were we to spend the night? Capt Alexander said he knew an old lady, a friend of the family, and he was sure she would put us up. We found her house and rang the bell. The door was opened very, very carefully. The days when the ring of the doorbell in the middle of the night struck terror into everybody's heart were scarcely past. Behind it was a frightened old lady – who was faced with a weird collection of people in the early hours of the morning, and asked to put up two ex-Belsen prisoners.

The name Belsen spelled lice, disease and God knows what else at the time. But you cannot turn people like us away, however threatening we might appear. It was a disagreeable situation for everyone concerned. Luckily, we had a good sense of humour and were able to sympathize with our host when she reluctantly led us into her sitting-room and swiftly removed all the cushions from the settee. She was obviously afraid of lice. She also only allowed us to use a small wash-basin in the loo. But who cared! We had a roof over our heads. Capt Alexander, his mission accomplished, bade us farewell. He had to attend to his own business.

10

Marooned in Brussels

'Phase one' was complete. We were in Brussels. Although we were on our own and did not have a penny between us, and our status in Belgium was not exactly legal, it did not worry us a scrap. In those days life was lived a minute at a time. The one thing we did have was the address of Hélène, 'la grande' Hélène, from the camp orchestra. I can still remember it: 26, rue de la Forge. We decided that Renate should stay put and that I should sally forth, on foot because I had no money, and try to find her house.

I had occasion once again to bless my father for insisting that we spoke French. After a minor odyssey through the streets of Brussels, I located the rue de la Forge and rang the bell. There was Hélène. I was welcomed with open arms. She had been reunited with her parents, who had managed to hide from the Germans. There was not a moment's hesitation. Of course I could stay there, even though they lived in a one-room flat.

We went to fetch Renate. We thanked the old lady for her 'hospital-ity' and returned to the rue de la Forge. Since there was no room to put Renate up there as well, we then went off to look for another friend from the orchestra, Fanny, and Renate stayed with her for the time being.

Our next move was to present ourselves at the British Embassy. We went there the next day full of confidence that this was a mere formality, and that we were going to walk out fully equipped with our magic permits to go to England ...

We sensed straightaway that something was wrong because we had the distinct feeling that we had been expected. That was peculiar. How could anyone have known that we were in Brussels, considering the unortho-dox manner in which we had arrived? We were treated with extreme courtesy and asked to take a seat. The man behind the desk had a letter spread out in front of him, and started to ask us questions about our plans for the future, our family, and so on. My eyes popped out of their sockets as I tried to read the letter on his desk, upside down. All I could see was the name 'Edward Lasker'. But that was enough. I understood at once what he was after. To refresh your memory: one of the qualifying conditions for being allowed into the United Kingdom as a Displaced Person was that you did not have any relatives in any part of the world apart from the UK.

The embassy official had to do his job, and that was to make sure that we fulfilled all the requirements. 'So you have no relatives outside the UK?' he asked. 'No, we have not', we answered. And then came what we had feared. 'What about your uncle Edward Lasker, the famous chess-player in America?' That was the cue for us to embark on a tirade about what a terrible person Edward was, and how we did not seriously consider him to be a relative at all since he didn't want to have anything to do with us.

Poor Edward. We maligned him mercilessly. While all this was going on, he had actually tried his best to get us an affidavit. The problem was that we had no desire whatever to go to America.

The reason Edward's name became involved was simple: Capt Powell, our well-meaning friend who had taken such excellent care of us after the liberation, had wanted to do us yet another good turn. He had written to the Passport Control Office in Brussels announcing our imminent arrival and requesting that we should be treated well, since we were such nice girls with a good family background – and, by the way, we were the nieces of the famous chessmaster Edward Lasker. He was not aware that instead of doing us a favour he had complicated matters. We could not really be cross with him because the thought behind what he had done was so touching.

The unpleasant truth was that the official was not able to issue us with the necessary papers since we did not qualify. He was very apologetic, and said that further inquiries would have to be made. He would let us know when a decision had been reached.

I wrote to my cousin Helli the very same evening:

Brussels, 25th January 1946

… What I feared without daring to talk about it has happened!!! We are in the depths of despair. 'Visas refused because of existence of uncle in America.' If Capt Powell had not written this letter we would have had the visas right away and we would have been in London on Monday night. What are we to do? We no longer fall into the category of people who have no relatives except in the UK. They questioned us about our uncle at the consulate, and we said he was ancient, way beyond sixty, does not know us, and has no money and no intention of helping us …

What they are doing there is making further inquiries about the uncle in question and to apply for an exception to be made in our case. We pray that the Home Office does not know about Edward's efforts on our behalf. If they do, we will be lost. By the same post Renate is sending a letter to Capt Powell asking him to contact Gordon Walker and you to try the Home Office from your angle again, since it might be an eternity before the British Consul here gets a reply, and our nerves are at breaking point. Please send instructions to uncle Edward as quickly as you can, even if it is not a very agreeable thing to have to do, saying that he must be prepared to state that he neither *wants* nor is *able* to do anything for us, should there be any inquiries. Do forgive us for piling everything on your shoulders once more. It is idiotic to be so near our goal and then get such a rebuff. What a terrible mess! We really are desperate. Please send us a cable when you receive this letter so that we know you are able to do something about it ... I curse the world and all its *bloody* regulations! That's enough for today, I am afraid.

Yours ever Anita

We were without papers, penniless and as good as homeless in Brussels, with nowhere to go. It was tantalizing to be so near and yet so far from finding a solution to our problems. After telling our family in England immediately about this latest fiasco, we then wrote to Edward explaining why we had said all those ghastly things about him, and asking him to forgive us – but at the same time to confirm our slanderous allegations if he should be asked any questions. I am glad to say that Edward was a good sport, and did everything that was required of him. He understood perfectly why we preferred to go to England. He was also probably relieved not to have had to take on responsibility for us.

Our second nerve-shattering period of waiting had begun, and the bombardment of the Home Office from every conceivable vantage point was renewed.

This is the moment for me to sing the praises of an organization like UNRRA. I have said that we had no money at all, nor did we have the ration cards that were still needed at that time. We did have a bed to sleep in (half a bed in my case, since I shared one with Hélène), but one needs more than a bed for survival. We presented ourselves at UNRRA's office and were given temporary identification papers, ration cards and some money without much ado. Vagrants like us were not unusual then and no one seemed surprised by our dilemma. The money we were given was just enough to get by with, and my cousin Helli in England also started sending us the odd pound note now and again in letters, which we were able to change into Belgian francs.

Time passed, and there was still no news of any permits for crossing the Channel. It was to take the Home Office all of three months to relent!

In the meantime we had to occupy ourselves in order to keep sane. I met many young musicians through Hélène, who was studying at the Conservatoire once more, and went to numerous concerts – sometimes to two in one day. That was possible because of my friends at the Conservatoire: I either had free tickets or paid a nominal amount for them. I had felt starved of music.

When it became clear that our sojourn in Brussels was going to be protracted, I got myself a cello teacher, once more by courtesy of UNRRA, and started to have lessons. We also had to find somewhere to live, and UNRRA was prepared to pay for that too, if we could locate something suitable.

It proved to be more of a problem than we could possibly have anticipated. As we knocked on the doors of various houses with rooms to let, we kept getting suspicious looks from prospective landladies who wanted to know whether our parents were aware of the fact that we were looking for lodgings. We were so young that they assumed we had run away from home. (If our parents had still been alive how delighted they would have been to know what we were doing!) After a long search, we were finally accepted by a landlord who seemed satisfied with our story, and we moved into a pleasant attic room in the rue de la Victoire. There were strict rules: we were to have *no* visitors, and I think we had to be home by a certain time. We did not care and were thankful not to have to abuse our friends' hospitality any longer.

My next pressing problem was practising. I was not allowed to do this in our room, or at Hélène's because she practised there herself. I tried practising at the homes of other friends, but the result was always the same: the neighbours complained. (I don't blame them.) A solution came when someone suggested I tried joining the University Orchestra. They were invariably short of cellists and would probably welcome me with open arms. They might even allocate me a corner at the University where I could produce my abysmal scraping noises in peace. I followed this advice and presented myself at the University, and was directed to a certain M Dufrasne (it is strange that I still know his name). He was the professor who ran the orchestra and, sure enough, he was overjoyed for me to join

Orchestre Symphonique de l'U. L. B.

Salle de la Cité Universitaire
22, Avenue Paul Heger
B R U X E L L E S

§

VENDREDI 1er MARS 1946
A 20 HEURES

Concert

donné avec le concours de

Saintpol Hou
PIANISTE

orchestre sous la direction de Georges Dufrasne

Brussels, March 1946. First page of programme for a concert given by the Brussels University Orchestra three days before I left for England as an outsider. He understood my problem and showed me a tiny room somewhere in the cellar, with no window, where he thought I would remain undisturbed and disturb nobody. I was over the moon with happiness. Every morning I took the tram from outside the Bon Marché to the University, and all went well for a while.

I struggled away in my airless cellar in the day, and attended orchestral rehearsals in the evening. Then the trouble came. I must have started my practising routine before term began, as I don't recall having seen many students about. All at once the door of my dungeon began to be opened frequently by students. They wanted to know what the hell I thought I was doing in there. It transpired that my cellar served as a convenient necking-place during term time, and that I was a grave impediment to the amorous pursuits of these unhappy, deprived students.

Since I had official permission to be there, and they didn't, we must have come to some compromise because I didn't relinquish my pitch.

I was quite enjoying my life in Brussels by then. I had made a lot of friends and had started to get a little younger, if you know what I mean. One of the highlights was when I found some money lying in the gutter. I could not believe my luck. It was probably the equivalent of a couple of pounds, perhaps even five. But it seemed like a fortune. What were we to do with such riches? We decided to throw caution to the winds and treat ourselves to a positively disgusting amount of ice-cream.

11

The Boat Across the Channel

At long last the day we had dreamed of came! We were asked to go to the British Embassy. The same man who had refused to give us permission to go to England before making further investigations, was sitting there behind his desk smiling and telling us that all was well. We could go ... We were dumbfounded. *Eleven months* after the liberation we had been allowed to go to England! I cannot remember how we reacted. We probably jumped up and down and hugged him. Now all we had to do was to buy some tickets. Yet again UNRRA did their bit and gave us the money that was needed. I believe they were paid back later on. We travelled to Ostend accompanied by as many friends as could come, and boarded the boat. It was 18th March 1946.

Renate and I sat down on the top deck and waited for it to leave. Suddenly we heard our names being called out on the tannoy. The announcement kept being repeated. 'Would the passengers Renate and Anita Lasker please report to the Captain's Office?' We were paralysed with fear. What could it mean? Was there something wrong with our papers? We decided to ignore the announcement and not budge from our seats until there was a reasonable amount of clear water between the boat and the shore. The boat began to move and when we were satisfied that the gap was big enough, we went off to see the Captain. We were totally mystified.

It turned out that we need not have been worried. But who could have blamed us for being on the lookout for more trouble! I am sure the Captain heard our hearts beating with fright. In the event, all he wanted to say to us was that he had been told that two ex-Belsen prisoners were on board ship, that he wanted to welcome us, and that we should call on him for help if there were any problems at Immigration on the other side of the Channel. We were speechless. Simple human kindness was not something we were used to, and we were deeply moved. We took it as a good omen for this new chapter in our lives and crossed the Channel with high hopes in our hearts.

Telegrams : ALIDEP, LONDON.
Telephone : CENtral 5272

*All communications should be
addressed to:—*

THE UNDER SECRETARY OF
STATE

Please quote the reference:—

L26025 & L26026.

Your reference:—

Home Office,
(Aliens Department),
10, Old Bailey,
London, E.C.4
12th June, 1946.

Sir,

        I am directed by the Sec retary
of State to express regret for the delay
which has occurred in answering your
letters of the 16th April and 15th May
and to say that he has decided to exempt
Renate and Anita Lasker from the special
restrictions imposed upon enemy aliens by
Articles 6A and 9A of the Aliens Order,
1920, as amended.   They should present
their Registration Certificates to the
Police in about a week's time for endorse-
ment.

                        I am,
                            Sir,
                    Your obedient Servant,

                    Jw Turness

Jack Sahrier, Esq.,
9, Warren Street,
W.1.

London, June 1946. Letter exempting us from restrictions imposed on 'enemy aliens'

We had no difficulties at Immigration. However, we were subsequently issued with an 'Alien Identity Book' which had the charming description 'enemy alien' printed on it. Can you imagine it? After all this, we had been classified as enemies! That we were in fact enemies of their enemy was too much for the average civil servant to comprehend. I was beginning to become extremely tired of constantly having to explain who I was, what I had gone through and, although German by birth ...

Jack, my English cousin, was so outraged that he stormed into the Aliens Department the very next day and the word 'enemy' was deleted from our papers with profuse apologies.

Our new life began then in March 1946. Not everything was wholly rosy, but it was the beginning of a return to normality and of a period of adjustment. For years we had lived in a jungle where physical survival was what counted. There was much we had to learn or re-learn, and there are many things that I never did re-learn.

I have never regretted for one moment that I came to England to start my new life. I have made my home here, and I have a great deal to be thankful for. But that is another story.

That brings me back to what I said at the beginning of the book. Survivors of the Holocaust are a race apart. However complete their re-integration into normality may be, there will always be an untouchable compartment which will remain the sole property of those who have mysteriously been spared against overwhelming odds. Words can never convey the abomination that took place in the name of cleansing the human race. My story has a happy ending, unlike that of millions of others whose existence was obliterated. There are no graves to testify that they ever did exist. Their stories will never be told.

How easy it is therefore for some people to deny this abomination. The millions who were murdered rely on those survivors to bear witness to their existence. To some extent that helps to expiate the guilt many of us feel at having survived.

Alas, it has once more become desperately important today to remind ourselves how precariously thin the dividing line is between human integrity and barbarism.

★

I did not have the joy of spending much time with my sister Marianne after my 'return'. As you will know after reading the letters from 1945, she had left England by the time we got there. I was to see her on two occasions, the first when she came back to England to visit us on what was meant to be an extended stay. She had to leave prematurely because the Home Office refused to give her permission to extend her visa. Some time later, I visited her in Israel. Sadly she died in 1952 after the birth of her second child. How ironic!

Appendix 1

Declaration of Possessions (Vermögenserklärung)

[Extracts from sixteen pages in the official German records meticulously listing every item of property in our household, with its value.

Before deportation, or possibly emigration, one had to declare every penny of one's wealth and every item making up the household goods one still possessed. The Gestapo then knew exactly what they would acquire when deportation was complete and they had rid themselves of the rightful owners, and were in a position to seize it.

This document is dated 9th April 1942, the date of my parents' deportation.]

[page 1]

Notice
Items which are taken away lawfully, need not be declared. [!!!]
A separate form must be filled in for every person. For minors or wives this must be done by the father or the husband ... All documents relating to money, etc., must be added.

Name: Dr Alfons Israel Lasker and Mrs Edith Sara Lasker, née Hamburger

Profession: Without profession ... formerly lawyer
Last occupation: Administration of property in individual cases
Address: Breslau 5, Höfchenstrasse 1, since November 1939
Name, address and possible affiliation to the Jewish race of the owner of the property:
Dr Werner Eschenbach, Breslau, Höfchenstrasse 1
Size of apartment, etc: Five rooms, one with balcony. Entrée bathroom, small closet, one cellar, one attic room. The main occupant Ernst Israel Schreiber, who moved at his resettlement, lived in one room, while the others were given over to three lodgers. I lived with my family in two rooms ... At present there are four lodgers in the apartment.
Value of rent: RM 135

8 — 8 —

IV. Wohnungsinventar und Kleidungsstücke (Anzahl und Wertangaben):

1. Möbel und Einrichtungsgegenstände:

   a) Schlafzimmer und

		RM.			RM.			RM.			RM.
__ Kleiderschrank	__		1 Sofa — Couch			3 Kopfkissen		60	__ Nachttischlampen		
1 Bettstellen	20		2 Sessel	100		__ Unterbetten			2 Stehlampe		40
Nachttische			__ Teppich			__ Daunenbetten			__ Frisiergarnitur		
6 Stühle (vk. m)	30		1 Bettvorleger		3	__ Steppdecken			__ Waschtischgarnitur		
__ Frisiertoilette			2 Brücken		50	__ Plumeaux			__ Wäschetruhe		
__ Waschtisch			6 Gardinen, Stores	70		2 Matratzen teils		40			
__ Kommode			__ Federbetten			1 Deckenlampe		15			

   b) Wohn-, Herrenzimmer:

		RM.			RM.			RM.			RM.
2 Schreibtisch und Sessel	50		__ Krone — Lampe			__ Schreibtischuhr			__ Bücher		50
			1 Schreibtischlampe	10		1 Schreibplatte		1	__ Lexikon		
__ Bücherschrank	✗		1 Stehlampe	40		__ Schreibmaschine			__ Weltgeschichte		
1 Bücherregale	10		__ Wandleuchter			1 Papierkorb		2	__ Prachtbände		
1 Tisch, groß	10		1 Stand-Wand-Uhr	30		__ Gardinen, Stores			__ Atlanten		
1 Tisch, klein	20		__ Spiegel			1 gleische	25	__ Globus		
__ Stühle			__ Teppich			1 Schr. Schr.	50	2 Üm —	
1 Sofa — Couch	40		__ Brücken			1 Vorhs.	25	Hr. K. gem.	30
__ Sessel			1 Schreibgarnitur	2		1 Arm...	30			

   c) Speisezimmer:

__ Eßtisch		__ Anrichte			__ Steh-, Wandlampe			Hausbar	
__ Stühle		__ Vitrine			__ Teppich			Gardinen, Stores	
__ Sessel		__ Sofa — Couch			__ Brücken				
__ Buffet		__ Krone, Lampe			__ Teewagen				

   d) Diele, Badezimmer:

1 Dielengarnitur	✗	1 Lampe	5		__ Schrank, klein		
1 Flurgarderobe	✗	__ Spiegel					
__ Läufer		1 Schrank, groß	50		__ Vorleger		

   e) Küche, Kammer:

1 Küchenschrank	✗	1 Kohlenkasten	3		__ Küchengeschirr zusammen		10	Vorräte, eingeweckt	
1 Anrichte	10	1 Lampe	1		1 Gardinen		3	Vorräte, weitere	
__ Besenschrank		__ Waage			__ Kühlschrank				
2 Küchentisch	10	__ Kochtöpfe usw.	10		1 eig. Gas-, Elektro-Herd		80		
1 Küchenstühle	1	1 Geschirr	6		__ Bügeleisen				
2 Leiter	5	2 Kisten	3						

   f) Kinder-, Fremdenzimmer, Salon:

Breslau, April 1942. Page 8 of the Declaration of Possessions (Vermögenserklärung) made out by my father the night before my parents were deported

Are you a lodger?: Yes. Of the above mentioned, Ernst Israel Schreiber has already moved out.

[page 3]

(a) *Children (including those over twenty-one years of age) who live in the household. Name, date of birth and possible members of the Jewish race*:
Renate Sara, born 14th January 1924: Jewess
Anita Sara, born 17th July 1925: Jewess
(b) *Children away from home. Ditto*:
Marianne Sara Lasker, born 28th April 1921: Jewess
Which children have an income?: Renate and Anita, RM 60 and RM 40 respectively per month in the Sacrau Paper Factory.
Which members of the family are emigrating with you?: My wife
Which members have already emigrated, and where?: My daughter Marianne, to England.

[page 4]

My total financial assets in this country and abroad are as follows:

[page 8]

Inventory of apartment including clothing (number of items and value):
[Here every item and its value is listed in detail. See page 147.]

[page 16]

I expressly declare that the information given is, to the best of my knowledge, correct, and in particular that I have not concealed any information about my possessions and financial assets ... I am aware that false or incomplete statements will be prosecuted.

Breslau, 9th April 1942

Signed:

Dr Alfons Israel Lasker
Edith Sara Lasker

Appendix 2

**Official German Documents Relating to
the Seizure of the Lasker Family's Property in Breslau**

[1] *Transacted in Breslau, 17th May 1942*
The Jewess Anita Sara Lasker appeared without being summoned. She proved her identity by producing Identity Card A 11450, issued by the Police President in Breslau, dated 20th February 1940, and declared:
(a) *My particulars*: My name is Anita Sara Lasker. I was born on 17th July 1925 in Breslau. I am a factory worker and my address is Höfchenstrasse 1 in Breslau.
(b) *My statement*: Before their evacuation in April 1942, my parents Dr Alfons Israel Lasker and his wife Edith Sara, née Hamburger, occupied a four-and-a-half room flat at Höfchenstrasse 1 in Breslau. My parents lived in one of the available rooms, my sister Renate Sara Lasker with her best friend Hanni Sara Herzberg in another, and I lived in the half-size room, while the other rooms were occupied by lodgers. Furniture and equipment in the rooms which are now occupied by me and my sister had been given to us by my parents for our personal use, and is regarded as our property.

Yesterday, officials of the Chief Financial Presidium came to register all items in these rooms for later confiscation. My sister and her friend and I work in the paper factory at Sacrau. If the expropriation of the contents of our flat goes ahead, we will have nowhere to live.

In my sister's name as well as my own, I request you to desist from carrying out the confiscation and to leave the interior of the rooms in our hands for our continued personal use. Furthermore, I request you not to seize the kitchen equipment which we also urgently need.

v.g.u. [read out, approved and signed]
Anita Sara Lasker
NN Customs Inspector

[2] *Breslau, 28th May 1942*
From the Chief Financial President
Lower Silesia
0 5205 – II/46

(1) To
Miss Anita Sara Lasker
Höfchenstrasse 1
Breslau

I am unable to comply with your request to release the objects in either of the rooms lived in by your sister and yourself or those in the kitchen.

(2) To NN to find out where the musical instruments (the grand piano and cello) from the Lasker flat have gone.
(3) Scholz to clear the flat.
(4) WV (file to be put back on my desk) on 10th June 1942.

By order
(signature)

[3] *Transacted in Breslau, 3rd June 1942*
The non-Aryan Miss Anita Sara Lasker of Höfchenstrasse 1 in Breslau, whose identity is known and is being examined, appeared at the office, and declared:

As far as I know, the musical instruments in question (the grand piano and cello) were the property of my uncle Ernst Israel Schreiber who was expelled on 21st November 1941 and in whose flat my family lived as sub-tenants. The grand piano was taken away from the flat with the rest of the furniture. I do not know what happened to the cello. The empty case is still standing in the hall and has not so far been collected. It is possible that the cello belonged to my uncle's brother, Hans Israel Schreiber, Telegrafenstrasse 3, and that he collected it.

I cannot add anything else that is relevant.

v.g.u. [read out, approved and signed]

Anita Sara Lasker
g.w.v. [transacted as above]
NN Customs Inspector

Gertrud Sara Freund
   Breslau 1
   Willmannstr.1/3
Kennkarte J Breslau
   Nr. A 04929.   Breslau,den 31.August 1942.

                    Dr.W. E s c h e n b a c h ,

                              B r e s l a u 5
                              Höfchenstr. 1.

Betr.Wohnung Schreiber-Lasker,Breslau,Höfchenstr.1.

   Als Vormünderin der Mädchen Anita Sara und Renate Sara L a s -
   k e r , Breslau,Höfchenstr.1,teile ich hierdurch folgendes mit:
   Die Grossmutter meiner Mündel,Frau Flora Sara Lasker,die mit
   den Mädchen in der obengenannten Wohnung wohnte,ist am 30.d.M.
   abgewandert. Nach der Abwanderung des eigentlichen Wohnungsinhabers,Ernst Israel Schreiber,hat sie die Mietslasten gemein-
   sam mit dem ebenfalls jetzt abgewanderten Untermieter Richard
   Israel Eisner getragen. Auch die Eltern der beiden Mädchen,
   Alfons Israel Lasker und Frau,die für den Unterhalt ihrer Kin-
   der sorgten,sind seit April d.J. nicht mehr in Deutschland.
   Meine Mündel,die in der Papierfabrik Sacrau mit einem kleinen
   Wochenverdienst arbeiten,sind nicht in der Lage,die Lasten für
   die Wohnung zu übernehmen.
   Ich bin daher gezwungen,die beiden Mädchen anderweitig unter-
   zubringen;sie werden ab Montag,den 7.September,im Jüdischen
   Jugendheim,Wallstr.9,wohnen.
   Die Jüdische Kultusvereinigung hat pflichtgemäss die oben ge-
   nannte Wohnung der Gauleitung angeboten,die die Räumung durch
   die Mädchen verfügt hat.
   Ihre Mietsforderung ist,mit Rücksicht auf die Abwanderung der
   letzten Mietezahler und des eigentlichen Wohnungsinhabers,bei
   dem Herrn Oberfinanzpräsidenten Niederschlesien,Hardenbergstr.
   9/11,unter dem Kennwort "Einziehung jüdischer Vermögen" anzu-
   melden,da diese Behörde für die Einziehung von Vermögen der
   abgewanderten Personen zuständig ist und demgemäss auch etwa
   bestehende Verbindlichkeiten zu übernehmen hat.
                     Ergebenst

                     Gertrud Sara Freund.

Breslau, August 1942. Official German document relating to Renate's and my removal to the
orphanage after the deportation of the rest of our family

[4] *Breslau, 30th September 1942*
From the Chief Financial President
Lower Silesia
o 5210 – II/46

(1)   To the
      Head of District Lower Silesia of National Socialist German Workers
          Party
      Eichbornstrasse 2
      Breslau 5

(1a) To the
      Mayor of Breslau
      Lodging and Lands Office
      Breslau

      re: Re-occupation of the flat of the expelled Jew Alfons I. Lasker,
      Höfchenstrasse 1, Breslau, sub-tenant
      The flat has been vacated and is now at your disposal.

By order
(initialled)

(2)   Office for registration in the list of vacant lodgings
      (done, initialled)
(3)   zdA (for the files)

[5] *Breslau, 1st February 1943*
From the Chief Financial President
Lower Silesia
o 5210 – II/46

To the Magistrates Court
Prison Department
Breslau

I herewith request that the Jewesses Renate Sara and Anita Sara Lasker,
who are in custody awaiting trial, should be summoned to the bearer of
this letter, Tax Assistant Kettke. They are to be questioned in connection
with the disappearance of objects from their former lodgings.

By order
NN

Appendix 3

Alma Rosé in Auschwitz

Extracts from 'A Doctor Gives her Account of Auschwitz-Birkenau'

by Dr Margita Schwalbovà
in *Eleven Women's True Experiences*

(*Elf Frauen Leben in Wahrheit: Eine Ärztin berichtet
aus Auschwitz-Birkenau 1942-1945*,
Plöger Verlag GMBH, 76855 Annweiler)

Auschwitz was a camp of absurd contradictions and insane inventions. One of its ironies was the music. The men's orchestra already existed when we arrived. It played for the commandos as they marched in and out of the camp.

The prisoners re-entered the camp in the evening, dishevelled and grey with fatigue. At the end of the column, on stretchers or borne on other people's arms, would be several dead comrades who had been killed – or had died a 'natural death'. From the stretchers hung feet and hands swaying rhythmically to the music. The newest German hits were played: 'Es war ein Edelweiss, ein kleines Edelweiss … hallerie, hallerie … '

The first attempt at making music in the women's camp was in the spring of 1943, and ended rather pathetically. Some girls played on a variety of instruments, without co-ordination and rather badly. Then a rumour spread that a new conductor had arrived and that the first concert would be held on Sunday. We did not quite believe it, but we went to listen all the same. Most people were free on Sunday afternoon. The concert took place between the Hospital Blocks, and the backcloth was blue sky.

The sounds that came from the violin of the new conductor were from a long-forgotten world … Who was this? The answer was: Alma Rosé. Alma had come with a French transport from Drancy where she had been interned for six months. She had been selected at the ramp together with several other women for Block 10, the block for 'guinea-pigs' where experiments were carried out ... When she heard an SS woman say that a violinist had come with the last transport and had obviously been gassed 'accidentally', she had not realized that she was referring to her. Her married name was Leuwen-Boomkamp and nobody had dreamed that it was Alma Rosé who was being talked about. She lived quietly. She could not adapt to the camp mentality and she suffered more from hunger than others did. One day the doctor in the block had her birthday, and the block-elder asked: 'Is there anybody who can play the violin?' Alma came forward and played that evening. It was a revelation for the inmates and for the SS. A few days later she was transferred to Birkenau as conductor of the Kapelle, the orchestra.

After a short period I had the chance to get to know Alma personally. She never understood the camp. She lived in another world ... She created a Kapelle mainly from girls who had been learning their instruments for two to three years. She did orchestrations for the orchestra, and practised excerpts from operas, etc, and from hit-songs . She was a very strict conductor and put her whole soul into the music. There was a concert every Sunday and they were great events for us. We looked forward to them the whole week. If it should chance to happen that an SS woman laughed or swore, Alma would stop conducting. It was sabotage. But Alma did not understand. She just breathed deeply and said: 'I cannot play like this.' No, they did not put Alma in chains. She remained a free bird in her feelings and her faith like a naïve child. She always thought that she would survive the camp. She believed every fantastic rumour that stemmed from the hopelessness of the inmates ... 'They will not gas people any more.' 'America has intervened.' 'Germany has been given an ultimatum.' ... I never had the strength to contradict her. 'After the war, I shall only play chamber music. Believe me, this is the purest form of music-making. I want to follow the tradition of my father ... ' The days grew shorter ... A terrible typhus epidemic broke out. Every day there were 200 to 300 deaths ... December 1943. Dr Mengele's tyranny overshadowed the camp. This insane psychopath was unpredictable in his moods and his deeds. When in the best of humour, he might make the most devastating 'selections' or give sweets to his favourite twins. Selections were made in the Revier and in the camp. The SS men were nervous. The typhus epidemic intensified, and they feared for their lives. Mengele sent a report to Berlin and awaited a reply. The condemned were put into two blocks. Approximately 7000 women. They had to wait between one and two weeks before they were killed. One can neither imagine nor describe such horror. A mass of half-crazed, starving and thirsty women in an airless room, waiting for death to come at any moment. Berlin did not reply. On the tenth day, Hoessler and Mengele made their decision and sent all these women into the gas chamber. It took two days. We heard the trucks ... the air was full of cries for help ... It seemed as though these events made no impression on Alma. Christmas was approaching. Everybody said that it would be the last one. Alma gave a Christmas concert in the Hospital Block ...

The year 1944 began ... Alma had retreated into her own world. The camp existed alongside her ... She trained the girls. The standard of the Kapelle improved from day to day; Alma worked from morning to night, orchestrating and searching for new repertoire ... 'Still not the right tempo ... the sound must be more refined.' 'Once again ... once again.' At night, she was half-dead. She stopped sleeping ... She did not see what was going on around her; her whole life was spent in a trance created by music. Her music.

The camp contained a great mixture of people. Apart from social misfits, murderers and thieves there were also political prisoners. Together with anti-fascists from every possible country, there were heroes of the Polish pogroms who were scared stiff of the Bolsheviks. These people began to intrigue against Alma. Alma was a Jew, and her popularity was growing from day to day. At first there was just talk behind her back, and then there was outright slander. She was called to the Oberaufseherin, the superintendent. She was accused of giving preference to Jewish prisoners, even when they played badly. She was accused of having her favourites and discriminating against others. 'Why didn't you accept the Polish violinist?' screamed the Oberaufseherin. 'Because she plays badly and is not musical.' 'You are lying', said the SS. 'It is because she is not Jewish. You will take her into the Kapelle! ... ' 'As you say,' replied Alma ...

Alma returned to the block and continued her activities; but she began to watch for hidden enmity in the eyes of her charges, to whom she wanted to impart pure music, and from whom she expected the uncompromising devotion that such pursuits demanded ...

'Blocksperre!', 'curfew!' ... [There follows an account of the gassing of the people from Theresienstadt who had been housed in the 'Familienlager', the 'family camp'.] I don't know how Alma got through that night. But I do know that she continued to play and desperately tried to escape from the inconceivable monstrosity of Auschwitz into the purity of harmony. She got through the day with a wounded, uncomprehending look in her eyes ... Early in the morning of 3rd April somebody came running to me and said that Alma had a high temperature. I hurried to her ... She was lying there with a headache and vomiting. She had a temperature of 39.4°C. No other symptoms ... 'What did you eat yesterday? ... ' 'Nothing special, but I admit that I drank some vodka.' I was astonished. Alma! She had told me once that she never drank any alcohol. Alcohol in the camp was nearly always methylated spirits. No change at lunchtime. After roll-call I returned to Alma. I froze ... Alma did not recognize me. She was deeply unconscious, and her temperature had dropped below normal. Her body was covered with small blue spots, and she convulsively gripped her head. The doctors were in despair. It was a bad case of typhus ... or perhaps meningitis? Or one of poisoning? Her stomach was flushed out. I held her pulse the whole time and applied cardiac treatment. Alma did not wake, even for a second ... She tossed herself from side to side. Her eyes were far away. The minutes ticked by slowly throughout the night ...

The girls brought Alma to the Revier. Her temperature was normal, but the symptoms of meningitis persisted. The blue spots were spreading. I sat with her and held her hand. The doctors could not understand it ... In the afternoon Alma was given a lumbar puncture. She was conscious and held my hand ... 'Alma, you will get better ... ' Cramp seized her hands ... Was it epilepsy? The attacks came more and more frequently. Hopeless attempts were made to save her. But nobody believed they would succeed ... I was left alone with Alma. It was raining. The doctors were trying to come to some conclusion about their diagnosis ... Alma, some people end their lives long before they die, and their extended lives are only an apparition. You took the last step two days ago ... and now you have found your eternal harmony ...

Appendix 4

**Transcript from the Official British Record
of the Trial in Lüneburg (ref. WO 235/14, Crown Copyright)**

Anita Lasker is called in.

The Judge Advocate: The witness, Anita Lasker, says she is a German Jewess and will give her evidence in English. She is taking the oath on the Jewish Bible.

Anita Lasker, having been duly sworn, is examined by *Col Backhouse* as follows:

Q. What is your full name?
A. Anita Lasker.
Q. Where did you live before you were arrested?
A. In Breslau, Street SA 69.
Q. After you were arrested were you eventually transferred to Auschwitz?
A. No, I had been in prison.
Q. When did you go to Auschwitz?
A. I had been one and a half years in prison and I left for Auschwitz.
Q. About what date would that be?
A. December 1943.
Q. Why were you in prison?
A. I was considered as a political prisoner.
Q. Which block did you live in when you reached Auschwitz?
A. I was living in block No.12, with the band.
Q. Did you see any selections for the gas chamber?
A. Yes, I saw many selections.
Q. Did you see any in hospital?
A. Yes, one.
Q. Who made the selection which you saw in hospital?
A. Hoessler and Dr Klein.

Q. How was that selection made?

A. People had to get up from the beds and pass by a few SS people. Among them was Hoessler and Dr Klein. The ones who did not look all right they put them on the side, and the ones who could live they put them on the other side, and after a few days the lorries came and picked the selected people up and brought them to another block, block No.25.

Q. How is it you saw so many of these selections?

A. I used to play in the camp band, and they made us play at the gate. The gate was just opposite the station. At the station arrived the transports and we would observe everything. The transport arrived, the SS people did the selections, and we have been just about fifty yards away.

Q. Was it or was not it [sic] well known what these selections were for?

A. It was well known what the selections were for.

Q. Was the existence of the gas chambers known in the camp?

A. Yes.

Q. Who was the commandant of the camp?

A. Kramer.

Q. Have you seen him at any selections?

A. Yes.

Q. What part did he take?

A. He was standing by the people and just showing the people who could go into the camp where to go, or where to go to the gas chamber.

Q. Do you remember some Hungarians coming to the camp?

A. Yes.

Q. When was that?

A. That was 1944; they started about May 1944.

Q. What happened to them?

A. There were so many people coming in the camp that nearly every night a queue was standing for the crematorium waiting for their turn. Most of them went into the gas chamber.

Q. How were the bodies disposed of?

A. I have observed that when these transports came to the crematorium it was not big enough, and they made big fireplaces beside the crematorium and I watched them throw bodies into those fireplaces.

Q. Were you eventually taken to Belsen?

A. I was taken to Belsen in November 1944.

Q. What was Belsen like when you first got there?

A. When I came to Belsen there were only tents with very few people in. No huts had been established.

Q. What were conditions like there?

A. Very bad conditions, because it was in the winter. It was very cold and the tents leaked. It was raining and the water was running in the tents. We also had to wash outside whenever there was water – which was only about half an hour in the day. It was very cold and we all felt ill.

Q. Who was the commandant then, do you know?

A. I do not know. I saw him very few times and he left very soon. I never heard his name.

Q. How did the SS behave to you then?

A. We saw mostly one or two Blockführers and they all had sticks in the hand, and to keep order they kept beating us.

Q. Did you have Appells there?

A. Very few in the beginning. The Appell started only when Kramer came into the camp. Then Appells started every day.

Q. About when did Kramer come?

A. He came about December 1944.

Q. Did that make any difference in conditions?

A. Yes, because when he came he started those Appells and we had to stay hours and hours in the winter, and he brought the Auschwitz order with him in the camp which meant beating and very strict discipline.

Q. You talk about bringing in the 'Auschwitz order'. What had conditions been like in Auschwitz, apart from the gas chamber?

A. It was very strict discipline in Auschwitz, and during an Appell everybody had to stay. Ill people had to get out and stay in the cold.

Q. You have told us that conditions went worse after Kramer arrived, but what happened towards the end just before the British arrived? Did that make any difference in the conditions?

A. Yes, just a few days before they arrived the SS people started to wear armbands with Red Cross on them. For instance, Dr Klein started to tell us that he will treat the people, and everybody had to be very kind with the ill people, but nobody believed him because we knew him from Auschwitz. He was obviously anxious.

Q. Did the approach of the British troops have any effect on the SS women?

A. Yes; Irma Grese, for instance, told me a few days before liberation that we must be very strong now. 'It will soon be the end and we will be liberated.' She obviously tried to mix herself with us.

Q. How had the SS women behaved before that?

A. They behaved very badly. For instance I know that Irma Grese used to carry a revolver or a whip, and the others as well have beaten and behaved very badly.

Q. Would you come down into the court here and have a look at the prisoners in the dock and tell us which of them you recognize and who they are? (*Witness does so.*)

A. No.1 is Kramer; No.2 is Dr Klein; No.5 is Hoessler; No.6 is Bormann; No.7 is Volkenrath; No.8 is Ehlert or Elase – I am not sure which; No.9 is Grese; I recognize No.10 but do not know her name; I recognize No.11, Hilde; No.40 (Gertrude Fiest) I do not know her name; No.41 (Gertrude Sauer) I do not know her name; I recognize No.46 Kopper; and I recognize No.48 Stenia.

Q. You have already told us about Kramer, Klein and Hoessler. What can you tell us about No.6, Bormann?

A. Bormann used to have a dog with her always. When she came into the camp we were always frightened. I have never seen her doing anything, but I know that everybody had a right to be frightened of her.

Q. No.7, Volkenrath; what about her?

A. She used to be the camp commander in Belsen. I have not seen her beating, but she was as well a member of the people who were responsible for the conditions in Belsen camp.

Q. Did you ever see her at Auschwitz at all?

A. Yes.

Q. What was her position at Auschwitz?

A. When I was there she worked in the parcel store; it was a place where all the parcels arrived.

Q. The next one you recognized was No.8 (Herta Ehlert).

A. She was second commander. She used to work together with Volkenrath in Belsen camp.

Q. How did she behave to the internees?

A. I have not seen her beating but she was always standing at the gate looking for something people were carrying which they were not allowed to, and she did her job very well. She was the right hand of Volkenrath.

Q. What about Grese, No.9?

A. I know about her that she used to carry a revolver in Auschwitz and a whip in Belsen, and I have heard about her that she has done a lot of shooting, but I have not seen it.

Q. What about No.10 (Ilse Lothe)?

A. I do not know anything about her, and I do not think she merits sitting amongst these criminals here.

Q. No.11 (Hilde Lobauer)?

A. I know her. I know that she was a collaborator with the SS.

Q. And No.40 (Gertrude Fiest)?

A. I have seen her ill-treating people when they were very hungry and tried to steal turnips. She made them kneel down in the snow eating them as dirty as they were, and to beat them together.

The Judge Advocate: Is this at Belsen or Auschwitz?

A. Belsen.

Col Backhouse: No.41 (Gertrude Sauer)?

A. I have seen her very often beating people with a whip as well. She was in charge of the kitchen; when she caught people stealing turnips she used to beat them.

Q. No.46, Kopper?

A. I have seen her very often in Auschwitz. She was known as the camp spy. Everybody has been frightened of her.

Q. Did you see her at Belsen?

A. She was there as well, but I did not see her there. I know only that she was there.

Q. And No.48 (Stanislawa Starostka)?

A. She used to be the Lagerälteste in Auschwitz and Belsen as well. She was a notorious collaborator with the SS and we have been much more frightened of her many times than the SS people.

Q. How did she behave to other internees?

A. She was very strict and the people have been even frightened to address themselves to her. She was just like an SS.

Q. What did she do to them?

A. For instance, when she saw you doing anything wrong – speaking with men or things like that – she would have gone and denounced that to the SS.

Cross-examined by *Major Winwood*:

Q. Was there an orchestra at Belsen?

A. No, only at Auschwitz.

Major Munro: No cross-examination.

Cross-examined by *Major Cranfield*:

Q. Did you go to the crematorium at Auschwitz yourself?

A. I passed once.

Q. Have you heard of the Sonderkommando at Auschwitz?

A. Yes.

Q. Was that accommodated separately from the rest of the camp staff?

A. They had a special block, but they had not been separated. Just a block of their own.

Q. Before the British troops arrived at Belsen did not a number of the SS go away?

A. Yes.

Q. Can you say approximately how many?

A. I could not. I know there were very many.

Q. Would it be more than half?

A. I think so, yes.

Q. Was there anything to stop the remainder leaving?

A. I do not know about that. I think so, because I heard that a few SS people who had gone already came back again and we heard that they could not go on as something must stop them, but we never heard about that exactly.

Q. Were you ever beaten at Belsen?

A. I was.

Q. Were you ever beaten at Auschwitz?

A. Yes, as well.

Q. Why were you beaten?

A. In Auschwitz there was no reason at all. We left Auschwitz to go to Belsen and we had been in the bath house and an SS woman just beat us without any reason with a big stick. In Belsen I have been late once and an SS man has beaten me.

Q. I want you to think of the most severe beating you ever had at either Auschwitz or Belsen.

A. Belsen.

Q. With what were you hit?

A. With a wooden stick.

Q. Was it a walking stick?

A. No, just a stick.

Q. Did you go to hospital as a result?

A. No.

Capt Roberts: No questions.

Capt Brown: No questions.

Capt Fielden: No questions.

Capt Corbally: No questions.

Capt Neave: No questions.

Capt Phillips: No questions.

Cross-examined by *Lt Boyd*:

Q. Were you ever in women's compound No.2 at Belsen?

A. No.

Q. You recognized No.41 (Gertrude Sauer) as working in one of the kitchens?

A. Yes.

Q. Which kitchen?

A. I think it was No.2.

Q. Do you know how often she worked there?

A. Until the last time she worked there.

Q. The last two or three days?

A. No, two or three weeks perhaps.

Q. Did she work every day during the last two or three weeks in that kitchen?

A. I cannot tell exactly. I did not observe if she came every day, but I think she did.

Q. You have said that you saw her using a whip to beat people?

A. Yes.

Q. I suggest you were mistaken and she only used her hand.

A. It may be that sometimes she used her hand but I saw her as well using a whip.

Q. Do you know if there was another SS woman very like her at Belsen?

A. I cannot remember now.

Q. Is it possible there was?

A. I cannot say yes and I cannot say no. I am not mistaken when I recognize her.

Capt Munro: No questions.

Lt Jedrzejowicz: No questions.

Col Backhouse: No re-examination.

(*The witness withdraws.*)

Index